Dismantling the American Dream

Dismantling the American Dream

How Multinational Corporations Undermine American Prosperity

Michael Collins

BEP

BUSINESS EXPERT PRESS

Leader in applied, concise business books

Dismantling the American Dream:
How Multinational Corporations Undermine American Prosperity

Cover design by Gregory P. Paus

Interior design by Exeter Premedia Services Private Ltd., Chennai, India

First published in 2022 by
Business Expert Press, LLC
222 East 46th Street, New York, NY 10017
www.businessexpertpress.com

ISBN-13: 978-1-63742-315-8 (paperback)
ISBN-13: 978-1-63742-316-5 (e-book)

Business Expert Press Economics and Public Policy Collection

First edition: 2022

10 9 8 7 6 5 4 3 2 1

*This book is dedicated to
my two friends Phillip Dickie and
Charles Roseberry who reviewed
each chapter of the book over a 5-month
period in many taverns and restaurants.
They patiently listened to my explanation
of the economic, political, and social
problems caused by multinational
corporations over a 40-year period. Their
comments, suggestions, and criticisms
are invaluable and led to many changes
in the text which enhanced the story.*

Description

I was a general manager of two manufacturing divisions for many years. We sold robots and other automatic equipment to the S&P 500 multinational corporations (MNCs) which gave me a chance to work closely with them, get inside their plants, and find out about their strategies. I have monitored the changes in their strategies since 1980.

This book is not an academic treatise. It is a concise story that tells what America's MNCs did to the U.S. economy and how they did it. It is an applied and actionable book which includes many suggested solutions that function as steps the reader can take in their company.

For instance, the primary target audience of the book are corporate managers and supervisors who are charged with the responsibility of carrying out the pledge made by their CEOs in 2017 to serve all stakeholders including employees, suppliers, and communities. To do this, they will need to understand the problems described in each chapter in terms of how the problem affects their company in terms of processes, technologies, finance, and markets.

I think this book would also be a useful guide for MBA students and graduates who are just beginning their corporate careers. They need to understand the strategies used by MNCs for the last 40 years, and why they made these decisions. Most importantly, they need to understand the corporate decisions that led to short-term profits, shareholder value, and outsourcing and how they affected the economy and millions of workers.

Another audience that really needs to understand the problems described in the book are the politicians who supported most of the multinational (MNC) decisions and strategies. Specifically, the Congressional men and women who voted and endorsed free trade agreements, allowing China into the World Trade Organization (WTO), and supporting the myth of the postindustrial service economy. These, in my opinion, were colossal mistakes particularly the belief that cheap imported products would somehow provide the average citizen with more money to spend in the service economy and lead to rising living standards. Congress is now debating a wide range of bills to address all of the problems caused by free trade and the import lobby, and it would serve them to really understand how America got into this economic jam.

In 2017, the MNCs made a partial admission that the strategies of the past have been detrimental to many of their stakeholders and they may be ready to change their strategies. To do this, the managers and MBAs in these corporations are going to have to understand how many of their strategies went wrong in order to develop new strategies to compete in the new economy and provide a foundation for implementing positive change.

Keywords

new deal laws; deregulation; short-term profits; outsourcing; economic inequality; reshoring; financialization; financial speculation; stock buybacks; five tax laws; tax reduction; postindustrial service economy; monopolies and oligopolies; free trade agreements; trade deficit; currency manipulation; overvalued dollar; shareholder value; productivity; gross domestic product; world trade association; decoupling from China

Contents

List of Figures

List of Tables

Preface

On August 19, 2019, 181 U.S. CEOs signed a commitment letter to lead their companies not just for the benefit of their investors, but "for the benefit of all stakeholders: customers, employees, suppliers, communities, and shareholders."

Alex Gorsky, the CEO of Johnson & Johnson, stated that this approach "better reflects the way corporations can and should operate today. It affirms the essential role corporations can play in improving our society when CEOs are truly committed to meeting the needs of all stakeholders."

Jamie Dimon, CEO of J.P. Morgan Chase, commented that,

> the American Dream is alive, but fraying. Major employers are investing in their workers and communities because they know it is the only way to be successful over the long term. These modernized principles reflect the business communities unwavering commitment to continue to push for an economy that serves all Americans.

Let me begin by saying yes, the American Dream is still alive, but it isn't just fraying, it has been dismantled by the policies and decisions of the multinational corporations (MNCs) during the last 40 years. Contrary to the language by Jamie Dimon, American MNCs did not invest in their workers and communities, and in the case of manufacturing, they laid off 7,500,000 workers and destroyed many communities from Dayton, Ohio, to Newton, Iowa, as they outsourced jobs and production to low-cost foreign countries. And yes, corporations should have played a role that would benefit society and all stakeholders, but they instead chose to favor their shareholders over all stakeholders and short-term profits over society and country.

Well, I guess you could say that their commitment is a breath of fresh air and possibly the first time CEOs from the major corporations have acknowledged that there are problems with stakeholders, particularly workers. So, the question is: What can corporate leaders do now to convince people that this is not just a public relations effort and they are really serious and want to make some profound changes?

I think that to begin this process of change to achieve these new commitments, they should first focus on what they did wrong since 1980 that didn't benefit their workers, communities, stakeholders, and society as a whole. This book provides managers of the 181 corporations a good summary of the problems and obstacles they will need to address and overcome if they are going to make good on their commitments.

CHAPTER 1

Introduction

The years 1940 to 1980 were good times for workers in general and American manufacturing. During this period, the United States experienced tremendous economic growth that built the middle class and launched the notion of the American Dream, where every generation expected to exceed their parents. Wages followed productivity gains and workers realized continuous gains in their income. In the America of the 1950s, a blue-collar worker could have a mortgage, support a wife and two kids, buy a car, and be the only worker in the family.

From 1948 to 1973, the corporations were sharing profits with labor and were paying people for the productivity they created. I think it reflects the fact that unions were very strong and workers had strong collective bargaining power. It was also during a time when corporations were not as driven by quarterly profits and were still supportive of their employees and communities.

But Things Began to Change

By the 1970s, America had 25 years of postwar growth, but the nation was facing rising global competition and corporate profits were being squeezed. The multinational corporations (MNCs) could have responded by improving product quality, protecting their technologies, and avoiding trade agreements that would sacrifice jobs, factories, communities, and manufacturing industries. But instead, they decided to reinvent their organizations, and the new emphasis was on reducing costs and short-term profits.

It began with the Milton Friedman doctrine in a 1978 article which said "An entity's greatest responsibility lies in the satisfaction of the shareholders." In the 1980s, the Business Roundtable translated this into shareholder value or "the point of a business enterprise is to generate economic returns to its owners, period." And so, shareholder value and short-term profits became the driving force at the expense of employees, communities, the economy, and country.

The Immediate Answer Was Outsourcing

To achieve their new profit goals, America's MNCs adopted a new business model that would do the R&D, engineering, and marketing in the United States, but do the manufacturing in a foreign country. The new model did provide better short-term profits and shareholder value but ran the risk of eventually giving the foreign contractors their technologies and markets. After 40 years of outsourcing to low-cost countries, America has lost 7.5 million manufacturing jobs since 1979, lost many supply chains, and closed 91,000 manufacturing plants.[1]

Outsourcing also led to the economic deserts in the Midwest. Cities such as Muncie, IN; Danville, VA; Dayton, OH; Bruceton, TN; Flint, MI; Johnstown, PA; Galesburg, IL; and Youngstown, OH, have lost thousands of jobs, businesses, and tax revenue and have never been able to come back.

The Decline of Wages

The knee-jerk reaction of most corporations was to cut labor costs anywhere possible. This meant the beginning of layoffs, frozen wages, temporary labor, moving employees to part-time status, and imposing two-tier pay systems in many of industries.

After Ronald Reagan was elected in 1980, the government sided with the big corporations and began to adopt policies that effectively forced workers to accept wage concessions, discredited the trade union movement, and reduced regulation of most industries which allowed most corporations to reduce labor costs even more dramatically. The Reagan administration also helped corporations by terminating the air traffic

---

[1] R.E. Scott. August 10, 2020. *Trump's Trade Policies Have Cost Thousands of U.S. Manufacturing Jobs* (Economic Policy Institute).

control employees and crushing their union, which began a lengthy period of union busting by the big corporations.

This was the beginning of a period where the U.S. workers compensation would not keep up with the growth in productivity. "During the last 40 years, the median weekly pay for Americans working full time has increased by just one-tenth of 1 percent per year and for men it has actually gone down 4 percent." The median income of full-time male workers is lower today than it was in 1975, while the costs of housing, health care, and education have increased by 50 to 100 percent. Average wages declined, employment at low wage service jobs increased, and inequality rose to the highest of all Western Nations (Figure 1.1).

The graph shows in the late 1970s, wages began to stagnate which were just a forerunner of some massive changes to the American economy.

Productivity growth and hourly compensation growth, 1948–2018

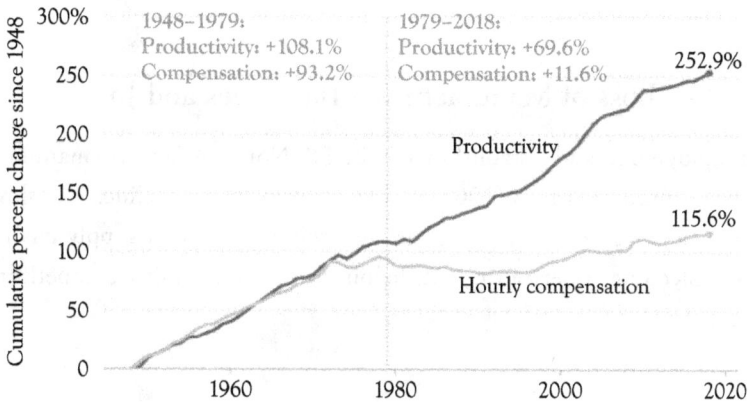

Figure 1.1 The gap between productivity and a typical worker's compensation has increased dramatically since 1979

Notes: Data are for compensation (wages and benefits) of production/nonsupervisory workers in the private sector and net productivity of the total economy. "Net productivity" is the growth of output of goods and services less depreciation per hour worked.

Source: EPI analysis of unpublished Total Economy Productivity data from Bureau of Labor Statistics (BLS) Labor Productivity and Costs program, wage data from the BLS Current Employment Statistics, BLS Employment Cost Trends, BLS Consumer Price Index, and Bureau of Economic Analysis National Income and Product Accounts. Updated from Figure A in *Raising America's Pay: Why It's Our Central Economic Policy Challenge* (Bivens et al. 2014).

The Pursuit of Free Trade Agreements

The biggest promoters of free trade agreements have always been MNCs. When they wanted Congress to pass a free trade bill, they always promised it would boost overall trade, create jobs, and give the United States access to more foreign markets. But in retrospect, FTAs such as the North American Free Trade Agreement (NAFTA) and the United States–Korea Free Trade Agreement (KORUS) have eliminated jobs and increased the trade deficit. The only real beneficiaries were American MNCs and their shareholders at the expense of American jobs, suppliers, and communities.

Free trade agreements have devastated our country's industrial base and the economic security of millions of Americans. Republican and Democratic leaders have systematically traded away manufacturing industries and the income and job security of American workers in exchange for promoting the interests of American international investors and the MNCs. In the 1992 Presidential Election against Bill Clinton, Ross Perot warned that that there would be a giant sucking sound as jobs and plants moved south of the border if NAFTA was passed and that is exactly what happened.

Loss of Manufacturing Industries and Jobs

Employment and establishments in 38 North American manufacturing industries from 2002 to 2020 continued to decline. The slow but relentless loss of manufacturing, technologies, and supply chains was bleeding America dry and helping all of our trading competitors to grow.

Financial Speculation

Instead of investment in plants, equipment, and jobs, MNCs invested in investments, many of them speculative for short-term financial gains. Wall Street guided hostile takeovers, mergers, and investments in foreign financial organizations. This became popularly known as the casino society. An example was that the volume of futures trading in stocks and bonds rose ninefold between 1973 and 1985.

Multinational Lobbying Power

Business decided in the late 1970s that if they were going to find ways to increase profits and decrease their costs, they knew that they had to buy access to Congress with lobbying money. Sector by sector, they began to build up large funds to pay lobbyists to get the crucial votes they needed.

Associations such as the National Association of Manufacturers, Chamber of Commerce, National Federation of Independent Businesses, and the Business Roundtable began by increasing membership and member donations. In 1975, only 175 corporations had lobbyists, but by 2011, they had 12,929 lobbyists who were dispensing an impressive $3.5 billion per year on lobbying. Political Action Committees (PACS) increased from 300 in 1976 to 12,000 in 1985.

None of these MNC accomplishments could have been achieved without the help of politicians—Democrats and Republicans. From the late 1970s on, lobbying was the key to get Congress and the executive to both get rid of New Deal laws and support all of the laws that would give MNCs, their shareholders, and the 1 percent, the increases in wealth they felt they deserved.

Transition to a Service Economy

In 1973, Daniel Bell wrote a book, *The Coming of Post-Industrial Society*, in which he described how the U.S. economy was transitioning from being a manufacturing-based economy to becoming a service-based economy. Bell's projection came true and we are now in the postindustrial service economy. The transition has been rationalized by most economists and academics who said that America can transition to a service economy and provide good jobs and living standards for the middle class. But it isn't happening. The new service economy is not producing enough livable wage jobs to maintain living standards. About 50 percent of the working citizens are being left behind.

Tax Reduction for the MNCs

The first part of the MNC plan to increase profits and wealth was to lobby Congress to reduce their taxes. The MNCs and their lobbyists were very successful in getting four tax reduction laws for corporations and their shareholders since 1981. They got another tax cut (The Tax Cuts and Jobs Act (TCJA)) in 2017 that reduced corporate taxes from 35 to 21 percent. In order to get the TCJA passed in Congress, the authors of the bill promised that the MNCs would invest the new savings in domestic capital investments and new jobs, but it did not happen. The MNCs used most of their new profits to buy back shares of their own stock to increase the share price and realize more short-term profits. To make matters worse, tax receipts have declined $160 billion since 2016 and $92 billion since the tax cut.

Monopolies and Oligopolies

Since 1999, the United States has undergone an enormous number of mergers and acquisitions (M&A), mostly by large corporations. There were 8,000 corporations in 1996, and by 2015 there were less than 5,000.[2] In most cases, the reduction was due to M&A, which has led to market concentrations. MNCs have formed monopolies and oligopolies that give them the power to control employment, wages, supply chains, consumer pricing, and market share.

Capitalism is supposed to be based on ubiquity of markets and competition, but since there have been few antitrust efforts to stop them, the MNCs have formed hundreds of monopolies and oligopolies in industries such as airlines, big banks, hospitals, meat packers, media companies, beer, autos, and oil and gas.

Losing Our Technologies

The MNC decisions to outsource production and build manufacturing plants in Asia, rather than in the United States, have given foreign competitors our technologies almost as fast as we invent them. New technologies and innovation are our only hope of competing in the world economy, but in signing technology transfer agreements and outsourcing,

---

[2]   L. Borsen, D. Brown, J. Grabow, and J. Kelly. May 18, 2017. *Looking Behind the Declining Number of Public Companies* (Harvard Business Review).

the MNCs are giving their competitors the products and know-how to take away their markets. It is a self-defeating and short-term strategy.

The Problem of Wall Street

The shift to shareholder value, stock prices, and stock buybacks by the MNCs is driven by Wall Street. The current financial philosophy of Wall Street is extractive not productive. They are not producing wealth by investing in goods, but they are producing wealth by financial engineering. Wall Street makes money by financing the trade deficit, from stock buybacks, and by investing in foreign capital markets which fund our biggest foreign competitors. Andy Grove from Intel said "the result is a high-profit, low prosperity nation."

Shortage of Skilled Workers

A 2018 study by Deloitte and the Manufacturing Institute predicted that U.S. manufacturing would have 2.1 million unfilled jobs by 2030. It is not well known that instead of investing in training, American MNCs are still opting for the short-term solutions of relying on immigration (H-1B Visas), outsourcing, and automation; but not investing in advanced training like apprenticeship to create the skilled workforce now needed in U.S. manufacturing.

Allowing China Into the WTO in 2001

The decision to allow China into the World Trade Organization (WTO) in 2001 was driven by the MNCs who wanted to build plants and move production to China. They wanted access to the growing China consumer markets, and they agreed to technology transfer agreements that would give Chinese competitors their technologies with the additional proviso to ship their products back to the United States. Allowing China into the WTO was all about cost reduction by importing rather than making products in the United States, and it was supported by the Clinton administration and free trade Democrats and Republicans. It accelerated the outsourcing of jobs and production and has resulted in a huge increase in imports, and a runaway trade deficit.

Trade Deficits, Currency Manipulation, and the Strong Dollar

The real score card that shows what is happening to the American economy is the trade deficit which exceeded $1 trillion in 2021. The MNCs ignore trade deficits and expect the government and taxpayers to continue to finance them ad infinitum.

The leading cause of U.S. trade deficits is currency manipulation and misalignment by China and 15 other trading countries. Currency manipulation happens when one of our trading partners buys up U.S. assets such as treasury notes, stocks, and bonds, which make the value of the dollar artificially high. Currency manipulation is illegal under the rules of the International Monetary Fund, but the rules are never enforced.

By making the dollar more expensive, it makes our exports more expensive and makes the foreign country's products cheaper. All treasury secretaries since 1994 believe a strong dollar is in our national interest because they believe that the benefits of a strong dollar are lower interest rates, more liquid financial markets, cheaper funding for American banks, and the ability to run large trade deficits.

Large corporations that import do not want the government to stop currency manipulation or to devalue the dollar because they want to keep import prices low. This keeps U.S. export prices artificially high and makes American products uncompetitive.

Shift in Wealth and Growing Inequality

Figure 1.2 shows that in 1929, before the Depression, the 1 percent owned 24 percent of total income of the country. By 1978, their share had declined to 8 percent of the total income because of tax increases on corporations and the wealthy along with comprehensive New Deal legislation.

However, in the late 1970s, the 1 percent and the corporations developed strategies to increase their share of the total income of the country. Figure 1.2 is based on a new estimate by the economist Edward N. Wolff in 2017. He showed that the 1 percent had increased their total share of wealth to around 37 percent, which is even higher than their share in the

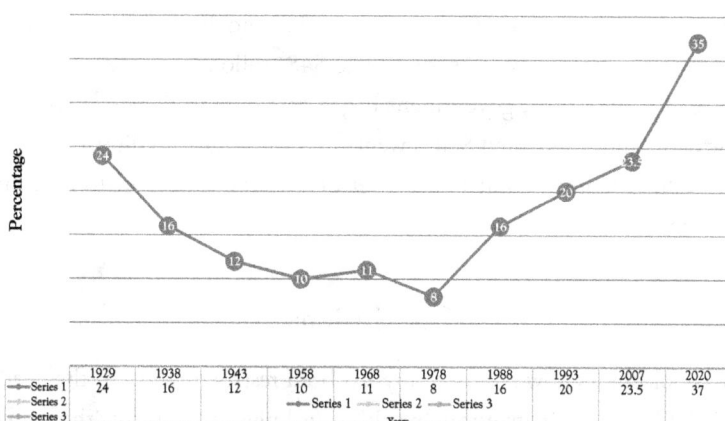

	1929	1938	1943	1958	1968	1978	1988	1993	2007	2020
Series 1	24	16	12	10	11	8	16	20	23.5	37
Series 2										
Series 3										

Series 1 — Series 2 — Series 3

Years

Figure 1.2 Top 1 percent share of total income

Source: 1929 to 2007, *Capital in the 21st Century*, Thomas Picketty, Belknap Press, 2014.

Source: 2007 to 2020, Wealth Distribution by Wealth Group, USA FACTS, Federal Reserve, September 21, 2020.

Gilded Age. The 1 percent have become $21 trillion richer, a sum almost the size of the U.S. economy.

What seems to stoke anger is that the tremendous gains in wealth by the 1 percent were at the expense of the middle class, which has led to the growth of inequality. Most taxpayers think that both the 1 percent and the MNCs have not paid their fair share of the economy.

Decline of Productivity and GDP Growth and the Increase in Debt

There are signs that show the American economy may be in decline. First, labor productivity, defined as output per labor hour, has grown at an average annual growth rate of 1.3 percent since 2005—well under the average of 2.1 percent going back to 1947.

There were several decades where the United States enjoyed 3 to 4 percent gross domestic product (GDP) growth, but since 2000, it has been an anemic 1.8 percent.

Another serious economic indicator since the 1980s has been the incredible increase in personal and business debt. In the face of falling incomes, consumers attempted to maintain their living standards by borrowing unprecedented amounts of revolving credit. According to Kevin

Phillips in his book *Bad Money*, between 1987 and 2007, "the credit market debt quadrupled from nearly $11 to $48 trillion."

At the same time, government began to amass trillions of dollars of new debt, and the United States went from the largest creditor nation to the leading debtor nation in a matter of decades. This shift to a casino economy is a house of cards.

Conclusions

This book shows how the economy has been restructured to fit the needs of MNCs and their investors, resulting in huge gains in wealth for the few. These gains have led to rising inequality while tens of millions of Americans find themselves unable to attain the standard of living of previous generations. More importantly, it shows how the growing power and control of MNCs have destroyed communities, industries and manufacturing and have put the future of the U.S. economy in jeopardy.

In the Preface of this book, I noted that 181 U.S. CEOs signed a commitment letter to lead their companies not just for the benefit of their investors, but "for the benefit of all stakeholders: customers, employees, suppliers, and communities." This book provides them with a chapter-by-chapter assessment of what has gone wrong for all of the stakeholders and what the MNCs can do to begin correcting the situation.

What has been good for them has turned out to be not good for employees, American manufacturing, communities, suppliers, or the middle class. MNC strategies for the last 40 years have led to the deindustrialization of America, which is slowly killing the economy and the American Dream. We are at a "now or never moment." It is time to find out if they can walk their talk.

CHAPTER 2

Outsourcing by Multinational Corporations

Over the last 40 years, the MNC's (multi-national corporations) commitment to short-term profits, shareholder value, and outsourcing has resulted in the deindustrialization of America. If these MNCs are really going to pursue their publicized "New Purpose," they will have to focus on reshoring jobs and industries and reduce outsourcing. So, it is now time for them to walk their talk.

In the 1970s, American corporations were suddenly confronted with serious international economic competition. The profits that the corporations had enjoyed since the beginning of World War II began to decline. This began an era of "corporate restructuring." Corporations began to focus on their core competencies and abandoned the large, integrated, corporate model to reduce costs and provide flexibility to management.

One of the primary strategies was to outsource their production to low-cost countries. Outsourcing took the form of reliance on foreign suppliers to manufacture components, the introduction of coproduction arrangements (joint ventures), and licensing technology including technology transfer agreements. It also began the move toward short-term profits and shareholder value and the slow hollowing of American industry. According to the Economic Policy Institute, American corporations have outsourced more than five million jobs and 91,000 plants since 1997.[1]

Outsourcing accelerated in the 1990s when the United States negotiated Free Trade Agreement (FTA) such as North American Free Trade Agreement (NAFTA) and Central American Free Trade

---

[1] R.E. Scott. August 10, 2020. *Trump's Trade Policies Have Cost Thousands of U.S. Manufacturing Jobs* (Economic Policy Institute).

Agreement (CAFTA), which reduced or eliminated tariffs. In the case of NAFTA, according to the Census Bureau, by 2019 our trade deficit with Mexico increased to $102 billion and $27 billion with Canada. A report from the nonprofit consumer advocacy group Public Citizen said the Trade Adjustment Assistance (TAA) program showed that 845,000 manufacturing workers had lost their jobs and applied for assistance because of NAFTA.

In 2018, General Motors announced they were closing five auto plants and laying off 14,000 people in the United States and Canada. This announcement caused me to flash back to another Ohio plant closure—the Ford assembly plant in Lorain, Ohio. Every time I went to Cleveland on business I stayed in Huron, Ohio, near Lake Erie. After I left the airport, my route took me through Lorain and by the huge Ford assembly plant. This plant opened in 1958, producing nine different Ford models through 2005, when it closed. With its huge empty parking lot, it was a stark reminder of what was happening to American manufacturing.

Mary Barra, CEO of General Motors, summarized the situation very well when she said, "I want to assure our owners that we are focused on creating shareholder value." Increasing shareholder value for corporations turned out to be a strategy of increasing the stock price, reducing costs, increasing profitability, and buying back shares of the company stock to make short-term profits. Contrary to what many people think, General Motors strategies had nothing to do with workers, families, communities, or the economies of states. It was all about shareholder value and short-term profit.

The auto industry is not unique in terms of plant closures. Other MNCs, such as General Electric, IBM, Caterpillar, Microsoft, Chevron, United Technologies, General Motors, Ford, Georgia Pacific, Harley-Davidson, Kimberly Clark, Briggs and Stratton, Honeywell, Merck, Pfizer, and Boeing, have closed or are closing American manufacturing facilities.

The Congressional Research Service confirmed that one of the primary incentives for outsourcing is to defer taxation on their profits made overseas until the earnings are repatriated. The deferral encourages U.S. firms to invest in countries where there are low tax rates. When congressional investigators questioned the wisdom, they were told that "patriotism just has to take a back seat to profit."[2]

One of the factors that seems to disturb workers who have been the victims, or fear they will become the victims of outsourcing, is the callous attitude by the MNCs and their associations. For instance, the CEO of the U.S. Chamber of Commerce praised the benefits of job offshoring and advised American workers to "let's not whine" about the practice. Carly Fiorina, then CEO of Hewlett Packard, said, "There's no job that is America's God given right anymore."[3]

Under the flag of the free market, the public found out that there was no loyalty to the United States. Instead of trying to protect American industries and slow down the rush to low-cost countries, the only real loyalty was to the short-term interests of their shareholders.

Donald Trump, when newly elected to office in 2016, was strongly opposed to outsourcing. Trump vowed to "bring back jobs" and to "make America Great again." During his four-year term, Trump increased tariffs and created a trade war with China. But he did very little to curtail outsourcing, as he had initially promised.

Joe Biden is now vowing to fix America's outsourcing policies in two steps:

1. Establishing a Biden Offshoring Tax Penalty and Biden "Made in America" Tax Credit, and closing the Trump Offshoring Loopholes.
2. Signing a series of executive actions to ensure that the federal government is using taxpayer dollars to buy American products and supporting American supply chains.

This means that Biden's Offshoring Tax Penalty is establishing a 10 percent offshoring penalty surtax and a 28 percent corporate tax rate. But, so far, Congress has not approved either of these tax measures.

---

[2] *Sending Jobs Overseas: The Cost to America's Economy and Working Families, Cornell University ILR School*, Report compiled by D. Marshall, AFL-CIO, Fall 2010.
[3] R. Konrad. June 30, 2004. "U.S. Chamber of Commerce Chief Endorses Offshoring of Jobs," *Associated Press*, Carolyn Said, op cite.

Isn't This the Way Capitalism Is Supposed to Work?

Capitalists and economists will make the argument that outsourcing and finding strategies that reduce cost and increase profit is not only how capitalism works but is the most efficient strategy used by corporations. The real question is not just what is best for corporations, but what is good for the nation, its citizens, its industries, and all of the corporate stakeholders.

A good example of what a Western nation can do to protect and grow its manufacturing sector and maintain jobs is Germany. Germany is protective of its manufacturing sector and does not have trade deficits, and they have trade surpluses every year. Their manufacturing wages are higher than those in the United States, and their manufacturing sector share of GDP is 18.8 percent compared to 10.8 percent in the United States.

The United States invented personal computers, robots, mobile phones, televisions, solar cells, and semiconductors, and then they lost the technologies when they outsourced them to foreign countries. A good example is the computer and electronics industries that are now controlled by Asian countries.

Outsourcing by American corporations has caused permanent damage to American workers, manufacturing, supplier companies, and the living standards of many families. It may lead to short-term profits for the corporation, but eventually, the corporation will lose the technology and the market to its foreign competitors. It is effectively handing its foreign competitors the rope to hang it.

Today, there are thousands of unfilled manufacturing jobs, and these jobs are projected to climb to 2.3 million unfilled jobs by 2030. It is no wonder that many manufacturing jobs are unfilled, and it begs the question why would any young person commit to a career in American manufacturing while U.S. corporations continue to outsource jobs and have no loyalty to country or communities. If American corporations are going to do something about unfilled manufacturing jobs, they need to decide whether their loyalty is to their employees, suppliers, and communities, or whether they have chosen to become "stateless" international corporations with no loyalties and only committed to short-term profits.

In a *BusinessWeek* article, Andy Grove former CEO of Intel points out that "250,000 employees of China's Foxconn company manufacture

Apple products, while only 25,000 Apple employees work in the U.S." The American job machine has broken down, he argues, presenting the danger of an unstable, unequal society that "consists of highly paid people doing high-value-added work" facing off against "masses of unemployed."[4]

A Gartner Survey released on December 15, 2021, found that 66 percent of logistics leaders increased their logistics outsourcing budget in 2021 and 74 percent anticipate an increase in the next two years. So, despite their claims to do more for their suppliers, communities, and other stakeholders, America's MNC's are going to continue to outsource job and production.[5]

The U.S. government bears a lot of the responsibility for reshoring jobs and ignoring the manufacturing sector. They have the power to take action against Chinese currency manipulation, dollar valuation, enforcing trade laws, taxing overseas earnings, and eliminating corporate tax deductions for closing American plants. But, so far, the government has favored the MNCs over American citizens.

Over the last 40 years, the MNC's commitment to short-term profits, shareholder value, and outsourcing has resulted in the deindustrialization of America. Outsourcing is like being overwhelmed by a snow avalanche. You can't stop it—you can only swim in the snow and hope to stay on top. I would like to make the argument that the United States should try a lot harder to swim in the snow and stay on top. We can't stop the MNCs from outsourcing, but there are many policies and strategies we can use to make it more equitable. We can enforce the trade laws, force the competition to play by the same rules, and stop giving our competitors the tools (technology and R&D) to ultimately win the global war.

---

[4] A. Grove. July 01, 2010. "Commentary: How America Can Create Jobs," *Bloomberg Business Week.*

[5] S. Hippold, Stamford CN. December 14, 2021. *74% of Logistics Leaders to Increase Outsourcing Over the Next 2 years.*

CHAPTER 3

A Surge in Inequality

A combination of events, including deregulation, tax reduction, the decline of unions, and a concerted effort to reduce labor costs by Multinational Corporations (MNCs), all contributed to the acceleration of inequality and the enormous gains in wealth by the top 1 percent. It hasn't been good for the country, the economy, or working people, so the question is what are the MNCs going to do about it?

I found a copy of an article in my library from *Scientific American* of May 1987 which I had saved for 34 years. It was by the economist Lester Thurow and is relevant because it was the first article that documented the beginning of inequality in America and what might happen in the future.

Lester begins his article:

> Since the late 1970s a significant and disturbing shift has been taking place in the distribution of income and wealth in the United States. The shares of total income going to different segments of the population have changed in such a way that the rich are getting richer, the poor are increasing in number, and the middle class has trouble holding its own. The trend can be described as a surge toward inequality.

He begins his statistical summary by saying that "from 1976 through 1985 the number of middle-income male jobs declined from 23.4 to 20.3% of the male workforce. The decline was even larger from 38 to 32.6% for males who work full-time all year." This was my very first documentation that white male workers with a high school education were in economic trouble.

Lester Thurow also made mention of GDP growth. He said "the rate of growth of the country's gross national product has essentially halved in the past two decades, from 3.8% in the decade 1960 through 1969 to 2% per year from 1979 to 1985." Lester also said that "the rate of growth of productivity declined by a factor of three, from 2.7% per year between 1960 and 1970 to 0.9% between 1979 and 1985."

At the same time, the growth of productivity in countries such as West Germany and Japan was from three to five times the U.S. rate. The lower productivity rates also directly affected wages. From 1960 to 1970, compensation to labor per hour work rose 2.7 percent per year. But, from 1979 to 1985, the compensation rate fell to 0.9 percent per year. Lester shows that of the 10.7 million new earners added to the economy between 1979 and 1985, 48.6 percent were paid less than $10,000 per year (in 1985 dollars).[1] The effort to reduce wages by the corporations had officially begun.

When Lester Thurow wrote this in 1987, it was the beginning of some major economic trends that would dominate the American economy and the fate of millions of citizens. It began with the MNCs outsourcing of production and jobs, followed by a long period of trade deficits, the decline of private unions, and the decline of American manufacturing. It also resulted in the rise of inequality and the decline of the middle class.

The Reduction of Labor Costs

In the early 1980s, the U.S. corporations adopted a program of "restructuring," which included reorganization of the company to lower costs and outsourcing low-skilled jobs to foreign countries. The restructuring also included a big investment in automation which began to eliminate blue-collar jobs. The introduction of the Internet and personal computers also gave corporations the opportunity to eliminate millions of white-collar jobs. Only recently is there some recognition by the corporations for what this has done to the middle class.

This was the beginning of a period where U.S. workers compensation would not keep up with the growth in productivity. Figure 1.1 in Chapter 1 shows what has happened since the late 1970s. From 1940 to 1973, the corporations were sharing profits with labor and were paying people for the productivity they created. It was also during a time when

---

[1] L.C. Thurow. May 1987. *A Surge in Inequality, Scientific American*, pp. 30–37.

corporations were not as shareholder oriented and were not as driven by quarterly profits.

From 1947 to 1979, the majority of working people did fairly well in terms of household income and wages. But after 1980, wages and household income began to decline or become stagnant for most of the middle class. Larry Mishell and Josh Bivens of the Economic Policy Institute said workers would be earning $10 more per hour if their wages had kept up with the increase in productivity.[2]

The poor wage growth of American workers was a *failure by design* driven by the MNCs and their shareholders. As Mishel and Bivens (2021) recently documented, wage suppression

> was generated by policy choices that resulted in excessive unemployment, eroded unionization, corporate globalization, lower labor standards (e.g., lower minimum wage), new imposed contract terms (e.g., noncompete), and corporate structure changes that pushed down wages and profits in supply chains to the benefit of large firms.[3]

These trends began in the early 1980s, after Milton Friedman convinced corporations that the sole responsibility of the firm is to maximize profits for the shareholders. MNCs bought into Friedman's doctrine and one of their primary goals was to reduce labor costs. This chapter demonstrates that their efforts have been spectacularly successful. As a result, wages have stagnated or fallen, while corporate profits and CEO salaries have reached new heights. If the minimum wage had kept pace with productivity over the last 50 years, it would be nearly $26 per hour today.

Two-Tier Pay System

The most insidious strategy to reduce wages was the introduction of the two-tier pay system, which also included a move toward temporary

---

[2] L. Mishell, and J. Bivens. May 13, 2021. *Workers Would Be Earning $10 More Per Hour If Their Wages Had Kept Up With the Increase in Productivity,* (Economic Policy Institute).

[3] L. Mishell, and J. Bivens. May 13, 2021. p. 1.

and part-time jobs. Generally, two-tier pay systems reward long-time employees—keeping their current wages and benefits—but reduce wages of all new employees.

This encourages older union workers to vote against younger workers to maintain their status and further erodes the union solidarity. Over time, as older workers retire and new workers are hired, the overall wage scale of the company declines.

Perhaps, the best example of the problems created by two-tier wage systems is United Airlines. Here's a chronology of what happened to United employees (and their formerly excellent service) since 1978.

The United Airlines Example

1978: Deregulation of the airlines.

1985: United Airlines demanded pilots accept a two-tier wage contract. Pilots strike but accept a modified agreement. Flight attendants also accept two-tier wage agreement.

1994: An employee stock ownership plan (ESOP) is negotiated that reduces wages 12 to 15 percent. Pilots accept another two-tier wage contract.

1997: Wage reopener—agreement to raise wages 2 to 3 percent was rejected. Passenger service agents join IAM union for protection.

1997: United negotiates a regional airline contract for a lower cost airline where employees are paid less than regular employees—United Shuttle.

2002: United Airlines (UAL) files for Chapter 11 bankruptcy protection and shifts 30 percent of its flights to lower cost airline TED. With bankruptcy, new labor contracts are imposed, reducing labor costs $2.56 billion per year over six years.

2002: The new UAL Chairman, Glen Tilton, tells employees to either accept his leadership decisions or he'll file for Chapter 7 liquidation. With UAL still in serious financial trouble, Tilton secures a $3 million signing bonus, $4.5 million in a pension trust, and $1 million per year in salary.

2005: UAL asks for and gets a second round of wage cuts of $200 million per year.

2005: Bankruptcy judge approves company plan to cut pensions and send them to the Pension Benefit and Guarantee Corporation, a government agency.

- UAL demands $96 million in additional concessions from labor from sick times, holiday pay, and by outsourcing its IT jobs.
- UAL emerges from bankruptcy after three years.

2008: The American Customer Satisfaction Index rates UAL next to last in customer satisfaction.

2010: UAL, still financially troubled, merges with Continental Airlines.

2012: Unhappy employees and disheartened managers contribute to United having the worst operational record in the airline industry. It has 77.5 percent rate of on-time arrivals, the highest number of delayed flights, and *more customer complaints than all other airlines combined*—according to the U.S. Transportation Department.

2014: United announces outsourcing 630 gate jobs at 12 airports. New nonunion employees will be paid between $9.00 and $12.00 per hour. Terminated employees will be asked to take early retirement, transfer to other cities, or quit. UAL says 30 more airports are targets for job outsourcing. Most bag and cargo handling jobs are already outsourced.

Since 1980, two-tier wage programs have been used in the airline, construction, electrical machinery, petroleum, printing, textiles, food, communications, health services, finance, insurance, steel, tire, wholesale, and retail industries.

Temporary, Part-Time Workers, and Subcontractors

Even though the two-tier pay scheme was a major factor in the decline of middle-class wages, there are several other job trends that were also significant contributors.

The Bureau of Labor Statistics Table A-8 shows that there were 20 million part-time workers in 2021 who worked less than 34 hours a week.[4] The problem is that part-time and temporary workers usually don't get any benefits. But perhaps, the real downside is that people with these kinds of jobs simply do not make enough money to support a family without using food stamps and other government support.

Contract Workers

In addition to part-time and temporary workers, there is another growing category—contract workers. These are full-time workers who are self-employed, receive no benefits, and pay their own taxes. From the corporate point of view, contractors are good because they don't have to give them a raise, don't have to pay their health insurance, and can use them only when they need them. The contractor has no pension and is not eligible for unemployment insurance.

A 2018 *NPR/Marist poll* found that "1 in 5 jobs in America is held by a worker under contract." They conclude that "within a decade, contractors and freelancers could make up half of the American workforce."[5] Workers across all industries and at all professional levels will be touched by the movement toward independent work—one without the constraints, or benefits, of full-time employment.

The Rise of the Gig Economy

The gig economy is a new definition for all nonfull-time jobs, which includes temporary jobs, freelancing, contractors, consultants, independent workers, and short-term jobs. The Harvard Business Review estimates that about 10 percent of U.S. workers rely on gig-type jobs which are about 15 million jobs. Contract workers might be the wave of the future as corporations continue to try to reduce their head counts. Some of the new gig jobs are hybrids that require technical skills and

---

[4] Bureau of Labor Statistics. September 2021.Table A-8, Employed persons by class of worker and part-time status.

[5] Y. Noguchi. January 22, 2018. "Freelanced: The Rise Of The Contract Workforce," *OPB*.

pay very well. But many are low pay and are contributing to declining or stagnant wages for the middle class.

Job Quality Index

In 2019, the unemployment rate reached 3.5 percent (a 50-year low) along with the growth of the stock market was interpreted by President Trump as "the greatest economy in the history of our country." But if you look behind the unemployment rate and stock market, it was obvious that something was fundamentally wrong and about 50 percent of the workforce was struggling.

A new monthly index called the Job Quality Index (JQI) shows a very different view of the economy. The JQI measures higher wage/higher hour jobs versus lower wage/lower hour jobs. Figure 3.1 shows that since 1990, job quality as measured by the income earned by workers has significantly declined. Less hours worked with less pay and little room for growth is becoming the norm.

The increase in low-quality jobs is a result of the growth of the service sector and service jobs such as hospitality, restaurants, and retail which pay lower wages. In 1972, 27 percent of all private industry jobs were low-quality jobs. Today, low-quality jobs are 59 percent of all jobs. In fact, since 1990, 63 percent of all jobs created were low-quality jobs.

Figure 3.1 *U.S. Private Sector Job Quality Index*

The JQI is important because the trend in private sector employment over the last 30 years shows that there is a decline in the capacity of many jobs to support a household—even those workers holding multiple jobs. A reading of 100 means that there are equal numbers of the two groups, while anything less implies relatively low-quality jobs. In October 2021, the JQI was 81.67 which means there are 81 high-quality jobs for every 100 low-quality ones.

The Big Shift in Wealth

During the 2012 Presidential Election, Republican Mitt Romney railed against Democrats and Socialists whom he said wanted to redistribute the nation's wealth and income. What he didn't mention is that wealth and income had already been redistributed, and he was one of the recipients.

Table 3.1 shows that wealth has been redistributed into a relatively few hands. It shows that the top 10 percent own 88 percent of the stock market and 91 percent of business equity. The top 10 percent own 88 percent of all investment assets leaving only 12 percent for 90 percent of all other investors. So, one can conclude that the top 10 percent are the shareholders of the MNCs.

Most working people feel the pressure of growing inequality but seem to be confused on how it happened and why. Figure 3.2 shows how the middle-class share of national income has been slipping for the last 50 years.

The gradual *shift in wealth* to the top 20 percent has been a redistribution of income and wealth at the expense of the middle class. Table 3.2

Table 3.1 Wealth distribution by the type of asset, 2013—investment assets

	Top 1%	Next 9%	Bottom 90%
Stocks and mutual funds	35.0%	45.8%	19.2%
Financial securities	64.4%	29.5%	6.1%
Trusts	38.0%	43.0%	19.0%
Business equity	61.4%	30.5%	8.1%
Nonhome real estate	35.5%	43.6%	20.9%
Total investment assets	50.4%	37.5%	12.0%

Source: Wealth, Income, and Power by G. William Domhoff, October 1, 2015.

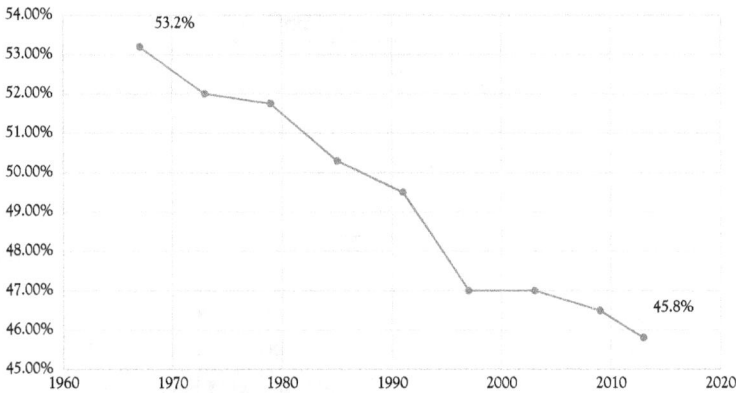

Figure 3.2 Middle-Class share of national income percent

Source: U.S. Census Bureau Share of income going to the middle-class 60 percent of households.

Table 3.2 Share of aggregate income shared by each quintile

	1980	2020	Loss or gain
Highest fifth	44.1%	52.2%	+8.1%
Fourth fifth	24.7%	22.6%	–2.1%
Third fifth	16.8%	14.0%	–2.8%
Second fifth	10.2%	8.2%	–2.0%
Lowest fifth	4.2%	3.0%	–2.2%
Totals	100%	100%	

Source: Bureau of Census—Table H-2 Shares of Aggregate Income.

shows the "big picture" on how the highest fifth of all earners did in the last 40 years. Table 3.2 shows that between 1980 and 2020, the top 20 percent of working people gained an 8.1 percent increase in aggregate income. I don't think that the average American begrudges the top 20 percent their income gains. What they resent is that the growth for the top 20 percent has come at the expense of the other 80 percent of working households.

Table 3.3 shows that in 2020, the top 10 percent of households had $85.83 trillion and the other 90 percent had $37.56 trillion. But the most startling number is that the bottom 50 percent of households had only $2.30 trillion.

This comes at a time when 46.7 million citizens are below the poverty level. Joseph Stiglitz in an oped article said,

Table 3.3 Distribution of wealth since 1989 in $ trillions

	1989	2020
Top 1%	$4.92 trillion	$38.95 trillion
90%–99%	$7.74 trillion	$46.88 trillion
50%–90%	$7.40 trillion	$35.26 trillion
Bottom 50%	$0.73 trillion	$2.30 trillion

Source: Distributional Financial Accounts—Board of Governors of the Federal Reserve System, 2021.

America is becoming a more divided society—divided not only between whites and African Americans, but also between the 1% and the rest, and between the highly educated and the less educated, regardless of race. And the gap can now be measured not just in wages, but also in early deaths. White Americans, too, are dying earlier as their incomes decline. This evidence is hardly a shock to those of us studying inequality in America. The median income of a full-time male employee is lower than it was 40 years ago. Wages of male high school graduates have plummeted by some 19%.[6]

The Economic Policy Institute says,

The growth of inequality is the central driver of the widening gap between the hourly compensation of a typical (median) worker and productivity. Specifically, this growing divergence has been driven by the growth of two distinct dimensions of inequality: the surge of compensation received by the top 10%—particularly the top 1.0% and top 0.1%—and the erosion of labor's share of income and the corresponding growth of capital's share.

Another way to look at the big picture is to go back to 1929 at the end of the Roaring Twenties when 1 percent of the wealthiest people had 24 percent of the total income of the country. After 1929, the nation fell into the Great Depression and the government answer was the New Deal where tax rates went up to 90 percent on the very rich and laws and legislation favored the average worker.

---

[6] J. Stiglitz. December 08, 2015. "Inequality Is Now Killing Middle America," *The Guardian.*

The effects of the New Deal lasted until 1978 when the 1 percent had only 8 percent of total income. But then, laws and legislation changed in favor of the wealthy again and they began to grow their income again. By 2007, they were back to where they left off in 1929, and by 2020, they had 37 percent of the total income of the nation.

When policy was oriented more strongly to sharing productivity growth more widely across income classes in the 30 years following World War II, typical worker's wages kept pace with productivity growth. When this orientation changed, wage growth for nearly all workers faltered. This highlights clearly that policy matters for the pace of wage growth for the vast majority. Mishel and Bivens of the Economic Policy Institute also show that a "rigging of the system" that empowered employers over workers was due to policy changes and changes in business practices that systematically undercut workers' ability to get higher pay, job security, and better-quality jobs—which generated wage suppression and wage inequality.

According to the Economic Policy Institute, the primary factors that explain 55 percent of the productivity–wage divergence were excessive unemployment, eroded collective bargaining, and corporate-driven globalization. They also identify additional factors, including misclassification, noncompete agreements, and supply chain dominance, which account for another 20 percent. This shows that policy choices drove the vast majority of the divergence between productivity and pay for the typical worker.

In the late 1970s, when wages began to stagnate, the middle class tried to keep up their buying power by women going to work, working longer hours, drawing down savings, and going into debt. But for many in the middle class, these coping mechanisms have been exhausted and no longer work.

Inequality and the Shift of Wealth

The great shift in wealth started in the 1980s, but really accelerated at the start of the Great Recession of 2008/2009. This shift has been a big factor in the decline of the middle class and the rise of serious economic inequality. The gaps between the haves and have-nots have widened at an accelerating pace (Table 3.4).

Table 3.4 Income, net worth, and financial worth in the United States by class in 2013

Wealth or income class	Mean household income	Mean household net worth
Top 1 percent	$16,439,400	$18,623,400
Top 20 percent	$257,200	$2,260,300
60th to 80th percentile	$76,500	$236,400
40th to 60th percentile	$46,000	$68,100
Bottom 40 percent	$20,300	–$10,000

Source: Wolff (2014); only mean figures are available, not medians. Note that income and wealth are separate measures; so, for example, the top 1 percent of income earners is not exactly the same group of people as the top 1 percent of wealth holders, although there is considerable overlap.

Yes, we are in the postindustrial economy, and the assumption that living standards will improve from one generation to the next is in question. There is no simple answer for why the rich got richer and the poor got poorer. A combination of events, including deregulation, tax reduction, the decline of unions, and a concerted effort to reduce labor costs by MNCs, all contributed to the acceleration of inequality and the enormous gains in wealth by the top 1 percent.

In an article "Wall Street is worried about inequality," the economist Josh Bivens summarizes the inequality problem very succinctly:

The way I see it, the rise in inequality that we've seen, starting in the 1970s and rising pretty steadily through the following decades, can be explained by a bunch of intentional policy decisions. The decisions have basically undermined the bargaining power of low- and moderate-wage workers and shifted that power to corporate managers and people who own capital.

If you are part of that 1 percent, life is good, and you're probably interested in supporting legislation that maintains your position. But if you are in the middle or lower class, or if you are in the 85 million workers (56 percent) of all workers who do not have a college education, then the future probably looks bleak, which has led to general unrest in working America. The society that was built from the New Deal—that propelled the middle class—has virtually ended.

French economist Thomas Picketty in *Capital in the Twenty-First Century* argues that "extremely high levels of wealth inequality are incompatible with the meritocratic values and principles of social justice fundamental to modern democratic societies." Furthermore, he adds that "the risk of a drift towards oligarchy is real and gives little reason for optimism about where the US is headed."

The majority of the shift in wealth and resulting inequality has been driven by the MNCs. It hasn't been good for the country, the economy, or working people, so the question is what are they going to do about it?

CHAPTER 4

The Myth of Free Trade

Despite the fact that most economists and many politicians love free trade, it has turned out to be unfair trade, and over the long term, I think it will be hard on corporations and the American economy. Free trade has been very hard on workers, manufacturers, suppliers, and industries and has inflicted pain on the weakest members of society, and the benefits have accrued primarily to the affluent and MNCs. Free trade has become a one-sided process where the benefits would flow to capital and the costs to labor. It is socialism for capital and free market for labor. For working Americans, it has become a race to the bottom.

Classic economic theory has always claimed that free trade delivers the greatest good to the greatest number of people: good for workers, corporations, shareholders, and the country. This idea has been accepted by both Democrats and Republicans for decades. The theory is based on the notion that according to "each's comparative advantage, countries can lift themselves out of poverty, and consumers can access affordable goods."

This chapter, however, makes the case that the winnings of free trade have gone mostly to the investors—the MNCs and their shareholders. Free trade has been very hard on workers, manufacturers, suppliers, and industries, and over the long term will be hard on corporations and the American economy.

What Most Economists Say

The economist Donald Boudreaux said that "free trade improves efficiency and innovation." He reasons that free trade, along with other market forces, shifts the workforce to "more productive uses, allowing more efficient industries to thrive" and bringing higher wages, infrastructure investment, job creation, and a more vibrant economy overall. What he doesn't say is that shifting the workforce to more productive uses for millions of workers meant shifting them into low-wage jobs or permanent unemployment.

The Small Business and Entrepreneurship council was even more supportive. They say,

> In the end, free trade reduces costs through the removal of trade barriers (such as tariffs and quotas); expands choices for consumers; keeps U.S. firms competitive; and opens new markets and opportunities for U.S. goods and services. Meanwhile, protectionism raises prices and limits choices for consumers; shields U.S. companies from competition—creating an environment of reduced efficiency, fewer innovations and inventions, and lower quality—and closes off international opportunities for U.S. entrepreneurs and businesses as other nations retaliate, resulting in slower economic growth and fewer jobs.[1]

Relying on Free Trade for Our Economic Future Is Based on a Myth

In a 1986 article *The Folly of Free Trade* by John Culbertson, he said "We have elevated the economic theory of free trade to the status of a national theology, and we allow its simple dictums as if they were immutable laws." Well, it is still true today but I think there are many fallacies, and when you examine it closely, it doesn't match up to the bold claims of the free-trade economists.[2]

First, economists will tell you that free trade is based on the economic principle of comparative advantage. It assumes that when a foreign competitor gains the upper hand, then the international value of the dollar will decline bringing trade back into balance again. But this doesn't happen in the current free trade market because the competitors game

---

[1] R. Keating. August 27, 2019. "Strong Support for Free Trade Among Economists and American Public," SBE Council.

[2] J.M. Culbertson. September 1986. "The Folly of Free Trade," *Harvard Business Review*, pp.122–128.

the system by manipulating their currencies keeping the dollar artificially high and the U.S. government bows to the pressure of the big importers and doesn't enforce our agreements.

Second, when jobs and production are exported to low-wage countries, the higher wage exporting country suffers cutbacks in production, job loss, and failures of supplier companies, which eventually leads to the market dictating that workers accept lower wages and reduced standards of living.

Third, as American companies continue to outsource jobs, production, and its technologies, Culbertson says the foreign manufacturer will gradually exploit the new knowledge and technologies by "capturing more and more of the product's value-added and eventually discarding the empty shell of the American business." This happened to the semiconductor industry which had to be bailed out by the U.S. government in the America Competes Act with $52 billion taxpayer dollars.

Fourth, another argument is that the United States has a responsibility to outsource jobs to poor countries by granting them our jobs and free access to our markets as a humanitarian gesture. This has proven to be a hypocritical claim because the blue-collar workers are sacrificed while the owners and investors get the spoils.

A Faustian Bargain

After four decades of free trade, it is now obvious that it is, at best, a Faustian bargain because in pursuing Free Trade Agreements (FTAs) since 1980, America had to sacrifice millions of jobs, increase the trade deficit, and accept the loss of technology, the decline of manufacturing industries, and the decline of middle-class living standards.

What Did Politicians Say About FTAs?

Clinton and NAFTA: By the 1990s, with the ascension of Bill Clinton to the White House, Democrats picked up the mantle of free trade. When NAFTA was passed, Clinton promised that NAFTA would increase the existing trade surplus, creating 200,000 new American jobs in its first two years and a million jobs in five years.

But, according to the Census Bureau, by 2019, our trade deficit with Mexico was $102 billion and $27 billion with Canada. A report from the Economic Policy Institute said that between 1993 and 2013, the trade deficits caused by NAFTA displaced 851,700 U.S. jobs.[3] The democratic party under Clinton had sold-out blue-collar workers and bought into the free trade mantra of the multinationals.

Obama on Korea: A renegotiated version of Korea Free Trade Agreement (KORUS) was signed in early December 2011 by President Obama. In a White House press release, Obama predicted 70,000 new jobs from the *bilateral* United States–Korea FTA he signed in 2011, but by 2015, the United States had lost 75,000 jobs. In addition, data from the International Trade Commission (ITC) showed that the trade deficit with South Korea went from $16.6 billion in 2012 to $25 billion in 2020.

Why Do Politicians Like FTAs?

President Barack Obama, when pushing for the Trans-Pacific Partnership (TPP) trade agreement, stated, "While some communities have suffered from foreign competition, trade has helped our economy much more than it has hurt." Economists argue that free trade stimulates economic growth and prosperity, and most politicians accept that a growing economy helps the party win reelection. So ever since NAFTA, Democrats and Republicans have believed the assumption that free trade and open markets lead to growth and prosperity—which in turn leads to greater electoral success for the party espousing free trade.

But with public pressure and the many problems that came out of NAFTA, politicians have been forced to rethink their commitment to free trade.

ITC Report

To really understand the outcomes of free trade, one must examine the winners and losers. There is finally a government report by the ITC in

---

[3] R.E. Scott. April 2, 2014. *The Effects of NAFTA on U.S. Trade, Jobs, and Investment, 1993–2013* (Economic Policy Institute).

June 2021 that analyzes the results of 16 FTAs from 1985 to 2020.[4]
The report is an attempt by the government to put a positive spin on
FTAs, but a careful analysis of the report shows little benefit and a lot of
problems. The overall takeaway is that there was very little growth or job
creation and most of the economic benefits went to the multinationals
and investors. Here are some conclusions from the ITC report:

1. FTAs were good for white-collar but not for blue-collar workers.
   The employment gains were 0.3 percent, and the biggest gains were
   for college-educated male workers (195,000) and college-educated
   women workers (150,000). FTAs have been very bad for blue-collar
   workers, particularly workers without a college education, women,
   and people of color.
2. It was good for big corporations like General Motors but not small
   or midsize supplier firms.
3. FTAs were very good for imports but not exports. Exports added
   1.6 percent and imports added 3.4 percent making the trade deficit
   worse. A rise in imports double the rate of exports suggests a net loss
   of jobs.
4. GDP rose only 0.5 percent between 1985 and 2017 and real income
   rose only 0.6 percent.
5. The Government Accountability Office found that there were limited efforts to enforce agreements and there were many labor rights
   violations.

Free trade increased trade deficits. Trade deficits began in the late 1970s
and have grown to exceed $1 trillion in 2021, an inconvenient fact largely
ignored by politicians and economists. According to the Economic Policy
Institute, trade deficits have eliminated nearly five million good-paying
manufacturing jobs and 90,000 factories.[5]

---

[4] K. Rapoza. July 09, 2021. "Government Shows Free Trade Deals Produced
Little Benefit, Except for Multinationals," *The USITC's report, Coalition for a
Prosperous America.*
[5] R.E. Scott. August 10, 2020. *Trump's Trade Policies Have Cost Thousands of U.S.
Manufacturing Jobs* (Economic Policy Institute).

According to the Department of Labor Statistics (DOL) by six-digit NAICS Industry annual averages, many important manufacturing industries are slowly dying. For the last 40 years, both Republican and Democratic leaders have systematically traded away the manufacturing industries and jobs of American workers in exchange for promoting the interests of American international investors and free trade. Here are just a few examples (Table 4.1).

Table 4.1 Industry losses in employment and establishments

Industry	Employment losses	Establishment losses
Textile mills, furnishings, and apparel	−256,909	−6,625
Paper, news print, and paperboard	−61,542	−157
Ferrous and nonferrous foundries	−59,688	−935
Machine shops	−32,039	−4,967
Computers and peripherals	−86,050	−290
Semiconductors	157,041	681
Motor vehicle parts	211,803	1,000

Source: Department of Labor Statistics (DOL) by six-digit NAICS Industry annual averages.

This is only a partial list of the 38 manufacturing industries which continue to lose jobs and establishments. Thirty-eight of the most important U.S. manufacturing industries lost 1,425,283 employees and 34,726 establishments by 2019. In the last 42 years, American manufacturing has lost 7.5 million manufacturing jobs. So far, the gain of $88.8 billion in GDP has been offset by massive unemployment and the devastation of middle-class families from Dayton, Ohio to Bridgeport, Connecticut.

Who Really Benefits From Free Trade and a Growing Trade Deficit?

1. First on the list of beneficiaries are the MNCs who have plants in Asia and get to export cheap products back to America: corporations such as General Electric, IBM, and Caterpillar.
2. Multinational retailers such as Apple, Costco, Wal-Mart, and Amazon, who get to import billions of dollars' worth of goods.

3. Wall Street firms such as Blackrock, Vanguard, and J.P. Morgan, which get to finance the loans we must have with our trading partners to finance our deficits, so that we can keep buying their products.
4. The real winners: The wealthy in all of the trading countries—not the citizens, workers, or manufacturers.

To accept, the philosophy of free trade depends on whether you accept the rise of trade deficits, increased import penetrations, loss of technologies, loss of industries, and jobs as a trade-off for minimal economic growth and prosperity. Economists and politicians have traditionally agreed with this trade-off.

Making these kinds of sacrifices is a noble sentiment, but it is based on hypocrisy. Why should the workers in the lower and middle class be asked to do all of the sacrificing while the multinationals and their shareholders gain all the spoils?

A basic assumption of FTAs is that everyone will play by the rules and allow the free market to operate. But the last 37 years of FTAs has shown that many countries who sign the agreements ignore the rules and use currency manipulation and other nontariff barriers to game the system. This problem has been exacerbated by the fact that the U.S. government has been unwilling to enforce the rules.

"Another assumption is that importing cheap goods with low prices is beneficial to American consumers, but the consumer that is paying less is an MNC be it Walmart or Ford." If the lower price point gets transferred to consumers at the expense of high-quality jobs, and a strong blue-collar market, then the positive (consumer price) is trumped by negative job loss.

In addition, keeping tariffs very low serves MNCs looking for cheaper supply chains to maximize profits.

The Opposite View

The author Roger Simmermaker says in his book *Unconstitutional:*

The idea that it is acceptable to outsource jobs and sacrifice manufacturing industries for the aggregate growth in the economy—or to import cheap products with a growing trade deficit because it best serves our consumers—is irrational. It is also irrational to believe that we can buy more than we can sell forever. It is possible for free trade to maximize the wealth of a minority of individuals and the global community, while it destroys the nation and its social stability.

He goes on to say,

Our 41 years of trade deficits have played a major role in the hollowing out of our manufacturing industries. We sacrificed the creation of our wealth, standard of living, tax revenues, and investment capital by transferring production to other countries by purchasing excessive quantities of imports.[6]

The only hope we have to save manufacturing is to change the idea of free trade and adopt a "fair trade" policy. To stop the decline of manufacturing, we need to consider the following:

1. What is missing is an equitable economic model that serves the majority. We clearly need a new economic model that protects workers and industries and stops the exploitation of low-cost foreign workers at the expense of Americans.
2. We need to build reciprocity into our trade. The former trade negotiator, Peter Navarro, has urged Congress to pass a Reciprocal Trade Act, which would allow the United States to impose reciprocal duties on all countries who have higher tariffs if they do not lower their tariffs and VATs.
3. To import all of the foreign products so that American consumers can have low-priced goods requires continually growing the trade deficit. You don't have to be an economist to reason that a country can't pile up debt faster than its income forever. The government is the only entity that can do anything about the trade deficit and

---

[6] R. Simmermaker. 2020. *Unconstitutional, Our Founding Fathers Rejected Free Trade and So Should We* (Consumer Patriotism Corporation).

needs to work toward a national goal to reduce the trade deficit and focus on balancing our trade budget.

4. We can't always depend on the foreign countries who finance our debt and keep the deficit game going.

5. If the Biden administration is really interested in growing manufacturing and establishing fair trade, they will have to stop currency manipulation which distorts trade flows and encourages outsourcing and the growth of imports.

6. The Trump tariffs with China are working, and we need to continue to use them to slow the flood of cheap imports and move toward a balanced trade budget.

7. Even though the multinationals have done well and have grown their profits using our current free trade system, I think the benefits are short term. Transferring their technologies and manufacturing to foreign countries is a game they won't win against unscrupulous countries like China who are dedicated to taking our technologies and replacing us as the world's super power.

CHAPTER 5

Innovation and the Loss of Technology

Everybody agrees that America's future economic growth and international competitiveness depend on our capacity to innovate, and the key to an innovation strategy is R&D. But what most people don't know is that manufacturing funds 70 percent of all private R&D and as manufacturing declines, so does the strategy of innovation. The only real hope for an innovation strategy is to stop the decline of manufacturing and protect the advanced technology industries which have been running deficits for 20 years. The government needs to do a lot more to protect the advanced technologies using national security restrictions or tariffs, and the multinationals need to reduce signing technology transfer agreements with their foreign competitors.

In 2015, President Obama said, "America's future economic growth and international competitiveness depend on our capacity to innovate." His plan, *The Strategy for American Innovation* also said, "Innovation-based economic growth will bring greater income, higher quality jobs, and improved health and quality of life to all U.S. citizens, and provide a multifaceted, common sense, and sustained approach to ensuring America's future prosperity."[1]

A strategy of innovation is a noble idea, but does not address the issue of losing the new products and technologies through outsourcing and technology transfer agreements. If new technologies are invented in the United States and then the manufacturing is outsourced to a foreign country, the inventing company eventually loses control of the

---

[1] The White House. October 2015. *A Strategy for American Innovation* (National Economic Council).

technology and the market. If we can't reverse this trend, then a strategy of innovation is a moot point. One of the most obvious examples is the semiconductor industry.

In 2021, the United States was faced with a shortage of semiconductors which interrupted the auto industry and many other manufacturing industries. It appeared that we were blindsided by the shortages, but this industry has been moving its manufacturing overseas for decades. U.S. chip producers account for half of the world's microchip designs, but only 12 percent of the global chip manufacturing. Why? Because almost all of them chose to outsource their production. In fact, Intel is the only U.S.-based manufacturer of microprocessors.

To explain what it would mean in the long term to lose industries, one need only look at America's technologies and inventions in the second half of the 20th century. America has been the source of new inventions for the world for most of the 20th century. The following is just a partial list of some of the inventions by the year they were patented: Microwave oven (1945), transistor (1947), defibrillator (1947), compiler (1949), bar code (1952), hard disk drive (1955), industrial robot (1956), video tape (1956), integrated circuit (1958), laser (1960), electronic spreadsheet (1961), light emitting diodes (1962), plasma display (1964), compact disc (1965), hand calculator (1967), laser printer (1969), charge coupled device (1969), microprocessor (1971), resonance imaging (MRI) (1972), global positioning (1973), mobile phone (1973), digital camera (1975), Gore-Tex (1976), personal computer (1981), Internet (1982).

The Problem

Unlike most of the inventions prior to World War II, most of the inventions listed above are no longer manufactured in America. So, American companies did the research and development of the original products, but then allowed them to be manufactured in foreign countries. The same process goes on today, but we are now not only losing the technologies but also losing whole industries. This scenario begs the obvious question. How many technologies and industries are we willing to lose, before we lose our ability to compete using innovation as our primary strategy?

Microprocessors are just one example of a technology invented in the United States but outsourced to Asian manufacturers. The semiconductor industry has lost 681 establishments (10 percent) and 157,041 workers (30 percent) since 2002 (Table 6.1). One of the big problems is that when the manufacture of semiconductors moves overseas, research and development goes with it. If the decline in semiconductors continues, the United States is in danger of losing its innovative edge in electronics and computers.

In an open letter to President Biden, Bob Swan, the CEO of Intel, asked Biden to pursue a manufacturing strategy for the semiconductor industry, which was bailed out by the federal government to the tune of $52 billion. So, one might ask, how did we get to this point in the semiconductor industry where the industry needs a bailout, and how many more outsourced industries will need the same?

Advanced Technology Industries

Semiconductors are part of a government designation called the advanced technology industries (ATIs), which are industries that are at the forefront of economic growth. The sector includes 50 industries: 35 manufacturing, 3 energy, and 12 service industries. They range from oil and gas to aerospace, biotechnology, life sciences, optoelectronics, communication, weapons, computer systems, nanotechnology, and software. These industries also include most of the disruptive technologies, such as additive manufacturing, advanced materials, advanced robotics, big data analytics, cloud computing, and the Internet of Things.

Why Are They Important?

ATIs are very important to the American economy because they are our best shot at maintaining competitive advantage against foreign competitors—especially China.

These industries employ more than 12.3 million workers or 9% of total U.S. employment. U.S. advanced industries produce $2.7 trillion in value added annually—17 percent of all U.S. GDP. That is more than any other sector, including healthcare, finance, or real estate. At the same time, the sector employs 80 percent of the nation's engineers; performs 90 percent of private-sector R&D; generates approximately 85 percent of all U.S. patents; and accounts for 60 percent of U.S. exports.[2]

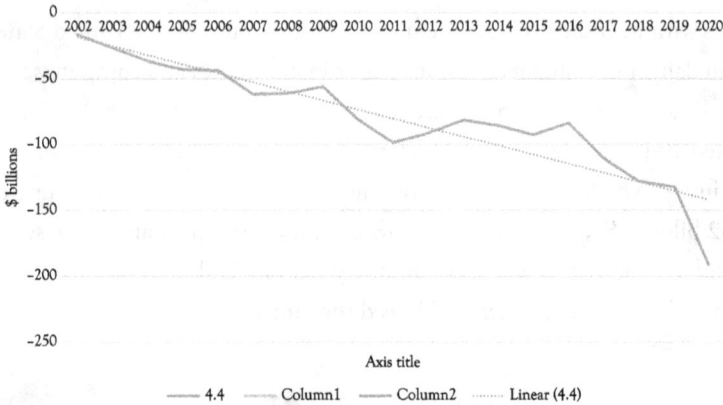

Figure 5.1 Trade in advanced technology products

Source: Census Bureau, Trade in Goods with Advanced Technology Products, U.S. International Trade Data, August 2021.

The ability to create these new technologies, particularly digital technologies, has implications for national security, economic growth, and the standard of living of most American citizens. You would think that the contribution of the advanced industries is so vital that the government would go all out to protect them as a vital national asset. But as important as ATIs are, there are big problems emerging. Figure 5.1 shows that America has been running trade deficits since 2002 (a total of $1.5 trillion in deficits over 20 years). In 2020, the ATI deficit was $191 billion, which was 28 percent of our total trade deficit in 2020. In 2002, the ATI deficit was only 4 percent of the total. So, why did this happen.

Why Are We Running Deficits?

The first reason for the deterioration of our advanced technology trade balance is the outsourcing of technology production. American

---

[2] J. Rothwell and H. Wial. February 06, 2012. "The Outsized Benefits of U.S Advanced Technology Industries," *Brookings Institute*, p. 2.

manufacturers do the R&D to invent these new technologies but then move the production to foreign countries to lower their production costs. According to Alliance for American Manufacturing, American high-tech companies that supply computers, software, routers, and printers such as Microsoft, Intel, Hewlett Packard, IBM, Dell, and Cisco "rely on Chinese factories for an average of 51 percent of the components used to make their products."

This is a problem for three reasons. First, their imports increase the deficit in advanced technology products. Second, it makes America susceptible to cyberattacks since we are relying on components made overseas. Third, it gives China and other foreign countries access to American technologies.

The Real Threat Is China

China has already swallowed the low-tech products we use to make. What they want now is our advanced technology products and production processes that were developed in the United States. The technologies they are after are all listed in their Made in China 2025 plan. China's primary strategy to get a hold of U.S. technology is to use joint venture and technology transfer agreements as a condition for companies to access Chinese markets. China also accesses our advanced technology secrets using security reviews of competitive technologies, product testing for safety reasons, acquisition of U.S. companies, and cybercrime. China's industrial policy is heavily dependent on fortifying their state-owned enterprises (SOEs). The United States and its partners should be a lot more aggressive in challenging subsidies of SOEs by using antitrust reviews for SOEs that eliminate competition.

Figure 5.2 shows the volume of imports of advanced technology products in 2019 by industry sector. The imports in these 10 product categories total $498 billion. The biggest ATI deficits are in information, communication, and telecommunications (ICT). Former President Trump issued an executive order to secure the ICT supply chain because purchasing these products from foreign countries is considered a national security risk. The executive order said that "foreign adversaries are increasingly creating and exploiting vulnerabilities in information and communications

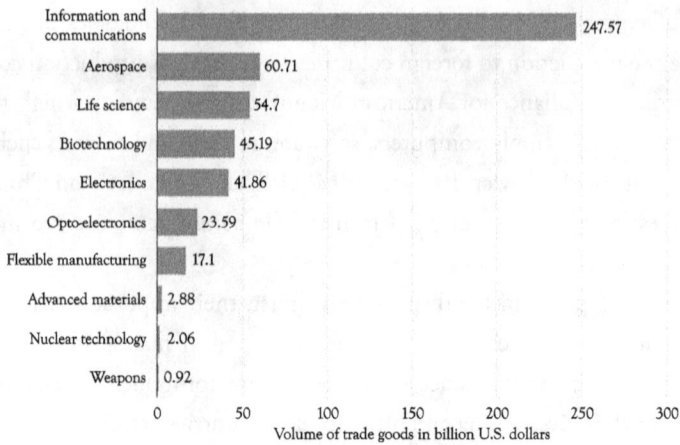

Figure 5.2 *Trade in information, communication, and telecommunication products*

Source: Wayne M. Morrison, June 23, 2019, U.S. China Trade Issues, Congressional Research Service.

technology and services, in order to commit malicious cyber-enabled actions, including economic and industrial espionage against the United States and its people." The order said that these actions "constitute an unusual and extraordinary threat to the national security, foreign policy, and the economy of the United States."

China is the largest foreign supplier of ICT equipment to the United States. In 2018, ICT imports from China totaled $157 billion or 60 percent of the total ICT imports. A May 2013 study by the Commission on Theft of American Intellectual property estimated that China accounted for up to 80 percent (or $240 billion) of U.S. annual economic losses from global Intellectual Property (IPR) theft.

We are losing the trade war for our advanced technology products, and we are losing it badly. The only thing that has offered some protections are the 25 percent tariffs under Section 301 of the 1974 Trade Act.

I began this chapter with a quote from President Obama about how a strategy of innovation was going to ensure the nation's prosperity, but neither he nor his economic advisers seemed to understand we can't have an innovation strategy without manufacturing. Seventy percent of our exports are industrial products not services, and the key to an innovation strategy is R&D and manufacturing also funds 70 percent of all private R&D.

In addition, the only real hope for an innovation strategy is to protect the advanced industries which have been running deficits for 20 years. To have any chance of reversing the current situation will depend on American MNCs and the government. The government will have to limit access to the advanced technologies using national security restrictions or tariffs. The multinationals will have to stop or reduce licensing arrangements that give their competitors easy access to their technologies who are likely to compete with them in the future and take their markets. They have taken a short-term profit approach and have ignored the long-term consequences to themselves and the U.S. economy.

CHAPTER 6

The Slow Erosion of American Manufacturing Industries

Despite a lot of talk about reshoring jobs and growing manufacturing, all administrations back to Bill Clinton have opted for free trade and watched 38 critical manufacturing industries decline in terms of number of plants and employees. Both Democratic and Republican administrations give lip service to stopping the decline of these 38 manufacturing industries, but other than the Trump tariffs, little has been done by the government to reshore jobs and production. This was a de facto decision to sacrifice manufacturing jobs and industries in order to import cheap consumer products.

I have been following manufacturing industries for many years (2002 to 2020), in terms of the changes in employment and establishments. Those people who think we might be in a manufacturing renaissance because of the digital revolution need to take another look. The data collected in Table 6.1 shows some inconvenient truths that 38 manufacturing industries are declining in terms of both number of plants and employees. The biggest problem, as shown in Bureau of Labor Statistics data, shows that seven of these industries are the critical industries that are fundamental to the manufacturing process and are absolutely essential if America wants to retain a viable manufacturing sector or rebuild the industrial commons.

Some of the industries, such as textiles, apparel, furniture, hardware, magnetic media, computers, cutlery, hand tools, and electrical equipment, have been declining for many decades and are probably beyond recovery. But the most perplexing of these declining industries are the ones that are fundamental to making other manufactured products. These are industries such as machining, machine tools, mold making, tool and die, semiconductors, forging, and foundries. It is difficult to see how we can ever achieve a manufacturing renaissance or maintain an industrial sector, while these critical industries continue to decline.

Machine tools: These are the master machines that make other machines and products. Max Holland wrote in his book *When the Machines Stopped*, "Thus at the heart of the industrial health of any nation is its machine tool industry. It is no coincidence that the erosion of the machine tool industry parallels the decline of domestic manufacturing."

In 1965, American machine tool manufacturers had 28 percent of the world market for machine tools, but today we have 7 percent of the world market. In 2019, the U.S. machine tool manufacturers exported $2.32 billion and imported $9.7 billion, according to Gardner Intelligence the research arm of Modern Machine Shop. This begs an obvious question: Can a manufacturing renaissance occur if most of the machine tools used by industry are imported?

Machine shops: Machining is a material removal process that is used on metal, plastics, wood, ceramics, and composites. Machining is essential to hundreds of industries and thousands of products as tiny as a machine screw and as large as a turbine bearing for a dam. Machining is absolutely essential for all industrial products but is also used in consumer products to make parts for everything from dishwashers and faucets to cellphones and toys. But, according to BLS statistics shown in Table 6.1, since 2002 the number of machine shops has decreased by 5,295 shops (21 percent) and employment has decreased by 64,342 people (20 percent).

Tool and die makers: Two classes of machinists that are critical to manufacturing are tool and die makers and mold makers. They are the highly skilled artisans that make the jigs, fixtures, dies, molds, cutting tools, and gauges used in the manufacturing process. To become a journeyman in either category requires four to five years and 8,000 to 10,000 hours of training. Since globalization began in the 1980s, Asian countries have gone all out to develop more tool and die, mold makers, and advanced machinists. In the United States however, tool and die makers have declined from 83,463 in 2002 to 55,694 in 2020, a loss of 27,769 workers.

Mold making: Table 6.1 also shows that industrial mold companies lost 1,334 shops (45 percent) and 10,481 workers (24 percent) between

Table 6.1 NAICS industry data on establishments and employment, October 2021

NAICS Code	Industry	2002 Establishment	2002 Employment	2020 Establishment	2020 Employment	Changes since 2002 Establishment	%	Employment	%
3132	Textile fabric mills	1,935	145,214	1,047	45,704	888	-45	99,510	-68
3141	Textile furnishings	3,261	116,429	1,694	43,209	1,567	-48	73,220	-62
3149	Other textile mills	5,141	77,956	4,698	57,383	443	-9	20,573	-26
31521	Cut and sew apparel	6,814	112,416	2,778	24,161	4,036	-59	88,255	-78
321911	Wood doors and windows	1,482	71,674	1,152	52,730	330	-22	18,944	-26
321918	Other millwork and floors	2,606	60,044	1,772	35,008	834	-32	25,036	-42
321920	Wood containers/pallets	3,549	60,371	2,999	60,534	550	-15	-163	3
322121	Paper (except newsprint)	637	106,423	429	49,704	208	-33	56,719	-53
322130	Paperboard mills	296	40,349	258	30,909	38	-13	9,440	-23
322211	Corrugated box manufacture	1,983	127,526	1,574	96,528	409	-20	30,998	-24
326121	Unlaminated plastics	656	30,038	501	21,816	155	-24	8,222	-27
326122	Plastic pipe and fittings	669	30,960	602	28,007	67	-10	2,953	-10
326211	Tires except retreading	168	66,375	167	48,599	0	-11	17,776	-27
326291	Rubber for mechanical use	626	48,505	469	28,785	157	-25	19,720	-40
326299	All other rubber products	758	31,744	676	23,013	82	-11	8,731	-28
327110	Pottery, ceramics, fixtures	1,645	35,593	757	13,376	888	-54	22,217	-62
327120	Clay building materials	830	36,176	652	20,787	178	-21	15,389	-42
327390	Other concrete products	2,647	62,512	2,097	53,448	550	-21	9,064	-14
33151	Ferrous, iron, steel foundry	1,124	99,452	737	53,077	387	-34	46,375	-47
33152	Nonferrous foundries	1,589	78,936	1,008	48,355	581	-37	30,581	-38
332710	Machine shops	24,773	315,856	19,478	251,514	5,295	-21	64,342	-20

(Continued)

Table 6.1 (Continued)

NAICS		2002	2002	2020	2020	Changes since 2002			
33211	Forging and stamping	2,703	11,968	2,230	8,850	473	-17	3,118	-26
3322	Cutlery and hand tools	1,748	54,448	1,322	34,683	426	-24	19,765	-36
33261	Hardware-spring and wire	1,861	70,891	1,281	39,981	580	-31	30,910	-44
333244	Printing machinery	591	15,890	408	6,371	183	-33	9,519	-60
33331	Commercial service machinery	3,117	128,503	3,060	85,124	57	-2	43,379	-34
3341	Computers/peripherals	2,164	246,993	1,890	159,293	274	-13	87,700	-35
3342	Communications equipment	2,715	183,072	2,442	85,523	273	-10	97,549	-53
3344	Semiconductors	6,670	523,680	5,989	366,639	681	-10	157,041	-30
3346	Magnetic media	1,822	55,707	1,022	10,936	800	-44	44,771	-84
333511	Industrial mold manufacturer	2,935	44,482	1,601	34,001	1,334	-45	10,481	-24
333515	Cutting tool accessories	1,448	30,764	1,062	20,914	386	-27	9,850	-32
333514	Tool and die and jig fixtures	5,288	83,463	2,839	55,694	2,449	-46	27,769	-33
333517	Machine tool manufacturer	2,171	43,711	2,051	38,200	120	-6	5,511	-13
3353	Electrical equipment	3,112	174,007	2,883	137,110	229	-7	36,897	-21
33522	Major appliance manufacturer	282	72,758	277	53,887	5	-2	18,871	-26
3363	Motor vehicle parts	6,765	728,766	5,765	516,963	1,000	-15	211,803	-29
371	Household furniture	19,472	398,687	12,635	226,458	6,837	-35	172,229	-43

Source: Bureau of Labor Statistics (DOL). Private industry by six-digit NAICS Industry annual averages.

2002 and 2020. The big question is, since a good deal of machining is now done overseas, is it possible to support all of the industries and companies who need machined products in the United States by only using foreign suppliers?

Foundries: The process of making parts by pouring metal to make a casting is ubiquitous and is used in the machinery, automotive, pipe, fitting, railroad equipment, valve, and pump industries. Castings are also used in everything from heart valves to aircraft carrier propellers and in every home for bathtubs, sinks, fixtures, and furnaces. Since 2002, the industry has lost 968 foundries and 76,956 workers. The primary driver of this decline is that most American corporations now buy their castings from low-cost countries where there are no environmental regulations and labor is cheap.

Forging and stamping: The contraction of the forging and stamping industry began in the 1980s because of import penetration. From 1979 to 1990, 25 percent of the forging companies in the United States went out of business. The contraction of this industry goes on today. Since 2002, this industry has lost 437 establishments and 3,118 employees. The demand for forging and stampings has been declining by the industry's major downstream markets, which include aerospace, agricultural machinery, and oil and gas machinery. Additionally, the world prices of steel and nonferrous metals have been volatile, making it hard for the industry to secure stable purchasing contracts. Most projections show that the forging and stamping industry revenue is expected to continue to decline.

Steel and aluminum: The Trump administration-imposed tariffs on imported steel and aluminum. This caused a big backlash from those companies who use foreign steel and from people who are afraid of a trade war. From a short-term perspective, the anti-tariff people are correct in that there will be more companies who use steel hurt by the tariffs than by those companies who make steel. But the real issue is longer term. If we continue allowing cheap steel into the United States eventually, we will lose the steel and aluminum industries just like we have lost furniture, apparel, and other industries—not to mention that these two industries are vital to national security and the military. President Trump got the world's attention on these issues with his round of tariffs. Perhaps, we might build on this momentum and find the political will to address the real problems.

Besides losing our technology and inventions to our competitors, we are losing skilled workers, the skills, the know-how, the suppliers, and the capital investment that come with investing into the production at scale. This is called the "industrial commons" by Gary Pisano and Willy Shih in their book *Producing Prosperity*. They make the argument that "investing in the industrial commons is not a matter of patriotism; it's a matter of good business leadership." I would add that America's MNCs have been the most responsible for losing our industrial commons.

Despite a lot of talk about reshoring jobs and production, administrations back to Bill Clinton always rely on their economic advisers to give them guidance on what to do about the decline of American manufacturing. Every administration starts out with a lot of rhetoric about how they are going to bring jobs back and grow manufacturing and exports. President Obama began his administration by setting a goal of doubling exports. But when he found that doubling exports required reducing the trade deficit and taking action on currency manipulation and the overvalued dollar, he abandoned the export goal. When it comes to developing an explicit plan with specific goals and objectives that might grow manufacturing, all former Presidents since Bill Clinton rely on their economic advisers and abandon manufacturing.

A good example was Christine Romer who was the former chair of President Obama's economic advisers who said to the *New York Times*, "that there is no compelling justification for policies aimed at supporting manufacturing." I think Romer's thinking is typical of most economists who don't believe that the trade deficit is a threat, or that we need to invest and protect the manufacturing sector. I think the same thing is happening with President Biden whose "Build Back Better" program makes vague promises about union jobs and manufacturing but does not offer a plan with specific goals and objectives, much less address currency manipulation and the overvalued dollar.

I don't think America has any choice but to find ways to save manufacturing and the American economy for the benefit of all citizens, workers, suppliers, and corporations. The alternative is to continue to allow our industrial base to shrink. If we are to find ways to protect the technology we invent, then the multinationals will have to step up to the plate and take a long-term view of what is good for them and the country. If America continues to lose jobs, technologies, and industries and keeps importing more and more foreign goods and services, we will become a nation of unemployed software programmers and service companies looking for someone to invoice. The future is now!

CHAPTER 7

Financialization and the Shareholder Revolution

The argument in this chapter is that financialization is not a good long-term strategy for the country or the economy. Financialization is about risky trading and the return on net assets that benefits its shareholders but not the parts of the economy that could lead to long-term growth.

Prior to 1980, the financial industry's role was to fund business and enable investment. But, over the years, a new financial strategy has emerged called *financialization*—defined as the "growing scale and profitability of the finance sector at the expense of the rest of the economy and the shrinking regulation of its rules and returns." It began with deregulation and slowly grew to create changes in tax, trade, regulatory, corporate governance, and law policies. Financialization is about shareholder value and short-term profits and is based on speculation, risk, and debt to enrich investors. This chapter shows how financialization and the quest for short-term profits have permeated all American corporations.

Figure 7.1 shows that the finance industry grew from 10 percent of GDP in 1950 to 22 percent by 2020. The disproportionate growth of finance diverted income from labor to capital. At its peak in the mid-20th century, manufacturing had 40 percent of all profits and created 29 percent of the nation's jobs. Today finance has 40 percent of the nations' profits with 5 percent of the jobs.[1] One of the big problems caused by finance rising and manufacturing sinking is that a high-employment industry was replaced by a low-employment industry.

---

[1] K. Phillips. 2008, *Bad Money; Reckless Finance, Failed Politics, and the Global Crisis of American Capitalism* (NY: The Penguin Group).

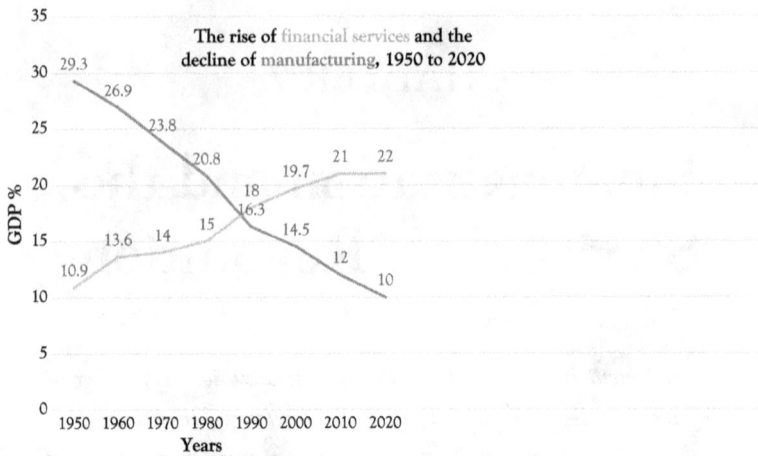

Figure 7.1 Changes in the share of U.S. GDP: 1950 to 2020

Source: Bureau of Economic Analysis—Value added by Industry as a Percentage of Gross Domestic Product [Percent], last revised on September 30, 2021.

This financial growth has led to a tremendous increase in economic and political power. The fact that Wall Street are the bankers of most public corporations has given them power over major sectors of the economy, especially manufacturing. Wall Street used to be the banks that once financed manufacturing and the capital investment and R&D that made America the best economy in the world. But after deregulation, Wall Street became the masters, demanding short-term profits over the strategies that led to long-term growth. Wall Street's demand for short-term profits forced most corporations to slim down their organizations and eliminate the functions that did not show a quick return on investment (ROI).

Financialism is totally about making money from money and has nothing to do with creating jobs or shared prosperity. In his article "Wall Street's Police State," Les Leopold says,

financial corporate raiders swooped in to suck the cash flow out of healthy manufacturing facilities. Wall Street, freed from its New Deal Shackles, loaded companies up with debt, cut R&D, raided pension funds, slashed wages and benefits, and decimated good paying jobs in the United States, while shipping many abroad.

Deregulation

Before getting into the results of the financialization of the economy, it is useful to show how the financial industry was able to remove or reduce most of the laws and regulations created during the New Deal.

The most important laws changed by deregulation were as follows:

1978: A successful legal challenge to state usury laws and the massive promotion of credit cards by the banks led to dramatic growth of credit card debt by consumers.

1978: Pension regulation was loosened which created a new market for speculation and the capital to feed it.

1978: Investors fled conventional interest-bearing accounts to alternatives such as money market, venture capital, and hedge funds which were lightly regulated.

1982: Congress passed the *Garn–St. Germaine Depository Institution Act* which deregulated the Savings and Loan industry. This led to speculation with other people's money and a crisis which would cost the taxpayer $201 billion.

1933: *The Glass–Steagall Act* regulated interest rates, established deposit insurance, and erected a wall between commercial and investment banking by restricting the former from engaging in nonbanking activities like securities and insurance.

1999: Congress, led by Senator Phil Gramm and President Bill Clinton, passed the *Financial Services Modernization Act*, which killed key parts of the Glass–Steagall law and allowed investment banks, insurance companies, and securities firms to consolidate through financial holding companies and use higher risk tools to gamble with the new money they had access to. This bill was passed as bipartisan legislation.

2000: Only a year later, Gramm inserted the new *Commodity Futures Modernization Act* into a must-pass budget bill that rocketed through Congress. One part of this bill would prohibit the regulation of derivatives which allowed finance gurus to leverage and speculate with other people's money. By using derivatives, credit default swaps, and other high-risk financial instruments, the big banks were able to chop up and resell loans and mort-gages as repackaged securities or derivatives. The new securitiza-tion became globalized and eventually affected much of the world economy.

2007: Speculation and lack of effective regulation led to the crash of 2007 and the Great Recession. The banking sector was bailed out by the tax payers, and the new regulations in the Dodd–Frank bill were not enough to prevent another crash occurring.

2010: During the bailout, the government allowed many of the big banks to use the bailout money to merge—Chase and Bear Stearns, Wells Fargo and Wachovia, and Bank of America with Merrill Lynch. So, the result is that they are much bigger today and have become an oligopoly that controls a huge amount of money. The 12 largest banks now control 70 percent of all bank assets. Derivatives are again backed by the FDIC.

2019: Today, the six largest banks in America have $10 trillion in assets underwrite nearly a third of all mortgages, control about 40 percent of all bank deposits, issue two-thirds of all credit cards, and hold 90 percent of all derivatives.[2] The industry is not afraid to do it again because they know no one goes to jail, and the government will bail them out.

The big banks and other Wall Street corporations are MNCs with offices all over the world. The problem is that the big banks have enor-mous lobbying power to buy off Congress and they are still too big to fail.

Growth of Debt

Debt is the lifeblood of financialization. It is where the finance sector makes the most money. Table 7.1 shows that since 1974, debt has had phenomenal growth in both households and businesses and shows that total financial and nonfinancial debt grew from $2.4 trillion in 1974 to

---

[2] Senator B. Sanders, May 23, 2019. *Senator Sanders Speech on Taxing Wall Street Speculation.*

Table 7.1 Debt outstanding by sector

	1974	1984	1994	2004	2014	2019
Domestic financial	$258	$1,052	$3,791	$11,868	$15,287	$16,001
Foreign financial	$81	$233	$443	$1,431	$3,284	$4,493
Total nonfinancial business	$821	$2,315	$3,830	$7,650	$12,044	$16,223
Total household	$680	$1,943	$4,541	$10,593	$13,915	$16,001
Federal government	$358	$1,364	$3,492	$4,395	$14,441	$19,056
State and local government	$208	$514	$1,107	$1,683	$3,089	$3,093
Total U.S. financial and nonfinancial debt	$2,407	$7,422	$17,205	$37,620	$43,489	$54,373

Source: Flow of Funds, D3: Debt Outstanding by Sectors, Board of Governors of the Federal Reserve, December 12, 2020.

$54.3 trillion in 2019. What is emerging is a new kind of speculative bubble based on consumer and corporate credit. In the last four decades, most of the increase in wealth went to the top 10 percent of all earners and the other 90 percent maintain their consumption by borrowing. There is a strong correlation between the rich getting richer and the other 90 percent going deeper in debt.

The debt picture has also changed for corporations. Corporate borrowing was around 4 percent of GDP between 1960 and 1990. Between 1994 and 2019, business debt rose from $3.8 to $16.0 trillion. Because of super low interest rates, debt is accumulating in oil fracking, student debt, BBB-rated corporate bonds, private equity firms, hedge funds, mortgage companies, institutional leveraged loans, and MNCs borrowing to finance stock buybacks. It is all reminiscent of the dot.com bubble in the late 1990s and the toxic mortgage bubble in 2008. Since the lifeblood of financialization is debt, it begs the question of has the financial sector set us up for another bubble or financial collapse?

According to the Federal Reserve Bank of St. Louis, "one of the major causes of the Great Recession was the excessive amount of risky debt in home mortgage markets and the resulting financial crisis." This has been exacerbated by the growth in recent years of auto loans and student debt with high delinquency rates.

According to the U.S. Bureau of Public Debt, in December 2020, the United States had a debt-to-GDP ratio of 128.1 percent.[3] This is a comparison of what a country owes with what it produces and is an indication of the country's ability to pay back its debt. A study by the World Bank found that countries whose debt-to-GDP ratio exceeds 77 percent for prolonged periods experience significant slowdowns in economic growth. Every percentage point of debt beyond 77 percent costs the country 0.017 percentage point of economic growth. As of 2020, America was 51 percentage points over the safe ratio. To put these figures into perspective, the U.S.'s highest debt-to-GDP ratio was 106 percent at the end of World War II in 1946. The higher the debt to GDP ratio climbs, the higher the risk of default. America is now a debtor nation sinking slowly into deeper debt.

Financialization and its emphasis on shareholder value and short-term profits are not benefitting the parts of the economy that could lead to long-term growth. Here are some examples.

Stripping Corporations: In an article in the Boston Review, Susan Berger a professor at MIT makes the assertion that, "Since the 1980s, financial market pressures have driven companies to hive off activities that sustained manufacturing." She gives the example of The Timken Company that was forced to split into two companies by the board of directors. The Chairman argued that the company should stay together because that is how it has been able to offer high-quality products with good service support. The board overruled him based on the potential of better short-term profits. This stripping down the company to their core competencies has been forced on most of the large publicly held corporations to some degree. But in stripping them down, many critical functions are lost. For instance, apprentice type training has been lost in many American corporations because it is long-term training and doesn't have a good enough ROI. Basic research, funding to bring innovation to scale, and diffusion of new technologies to suppliers have also been dropped or reduced because they are seen by the shareholders as being peripheral to the core competencies.

---

[3] The White House, Office of Management and Budget. December 2020. *United States Recorded Government Debt of 128.10 percent of GDP in 2020.*

Capital Investment: Research from the Roosevelt Institute shows that productive corporate investment disappeared in the last 30 years and has been replaced by shareholder payouts. They say, "Whereas firms once borrowed to invest and improve their long-term performance, they now borrow to enrich their investors in the short-run." The research showed that "In the 1960s and 1970s, an additional dollar of earnings or borrowing was associated with about a 40-cent increase in investment. Since the 1980s, less than 10 cents of each borrowed dollar is invested."[4]

If we are going to be competitive in the world, then we must promote the manufacturing sector and continue to invest in the research and manufacturing of the new technologies and products that will allow the United States to compete. This means investing in capital equipment, research and development, basic science research, and start-up companies for the long term. This won't happen as long as the financial sector is in charge.

Innovation and R&D: Most politicians today agree that innovation is the key strategy that will keep America in the race and its position as global leader. Innovation comes from research and development, and more than 70 percent of all private sectors' R&D comes from manufacturing. So, this is the same problem as capital investments mentioned earlier and begs the same question—how can innovation and new technologies happen without long-term financial support? And as the Roosevelt Institute found, how will there be enough money for R&D investment if most of the money is flowing out to shareholders in the form of dividends and stock buybacks. At this point, Wall Street has the upper hand and continues to focus on short-term profits rather than investing in manufacturing and the R&D that leads to innovation.

If we are going to have a chance at reversing the decline of manufacturing or developing a strategy of innovation that will keep us competitive, the current direction of the financial industry must be changed. In their pursuit of short-term profits, they are jeopardizing the long-term health of the economy and the manufacturing sector.

---

[4] J.W. Mason. May 2015. *Disgorge the Cash, The Disconnect Between Corporate Borrowing and Investment* (The Roosevelt Institute).

A decline in start-up companies: "The rate of company formation is half of what it was four decades ago," says a February 2018 *New York Times* article.[5] The innovation that start-ups bring is particularly important to manufacturing and high tech, which rely on new ideas, technologies, and increased productivity for long-term growth. The article said, "Researchers found that the decline in companies entering the market since 1980 has trimmed productivity growth by about 3.1 percent." I think this decline has happened because of the U.S. financial industry's change in focus from lending to speculation. Many start-ups must now go overseas to get the second round of funding to expand.

Financialization has hurt the American economy, and the symptoms are as follows:

1. Rising inequality
2. Stagnant wages
3. Falling productivity
4. The decline of GDP growth
5. Lack of regulation
6. The decline of innovation
7. Decline of capital investment
8. Short-term planning over long-term planning

Supporters of financialization make the case that financialization is the final or perfect form of Free-Market Capitalism (FMC) where profits are realized the quickest, costs are minimized, and the government is not allowed to interfere in the process. Financialization is about making short-term profits and cutting costs to satisfy high-risk investors looking for quick returns.

The argument in this chapter is that financialization is not a good long-term strategy for the country or the economy. There is no coincidence that the rise of financialization has happened during the decline of manufacturing, middle-class income, and capital investment or during the rise of inequality. It is also no coincidence that during the same period,

---

[5] E. Porter. February 06, 2018. *Where Are the Start-Ups? Loss of Dynamism Is Impeding Growth* (New York Times).

there was an enormous shift in wealth to the top 20 percent earners at the expense of the bottom 80 percent.

The choice is clear, either we push for more regulation of the financial industry like we did during the New Deal or they will eventually destroy both themselves and the economy. William Banzai put the big bank problem in perspective when he said, "If we don't get rid of the incentive to loot, then the only question is what form the next round of looting will take."

CHAPTER 8

The Threat of Wall Street

The Nobel prize winning economist James Tobin summarized the emerging problems of Wall Street back in 1984. He said "Very little of the work done by the securities industry … has to do with financing of real investment." Instead of doing the creative work of establishing real assets through investment, Wall Street is doing distributive work of financial assets which is moving wealth from one source to another. "They are engaged in distributing wealth not creating it."[1]

The shift in the economy that began during the Reagan era is all about short-term strategies to make fast profits. Economic analyst Rana Foroohar makes the case that the U.S. system of market capitalism itself is broken. She says "that the finance sector of the economy, which includes banking, insurance, real estate, hedge funds and mutual funds, used to be the servant of business, in which they took individual and corporate savings and funneled the money into productive enterprises."[2] Foroohar thinks that the "financialization of America is perpetuating Wall Street's reign over Main Street, widening the gap between rich and poor, and threatening the American Dream."

After deregulation, Wall Street became the masters of nonfinancial businesses, demanding short-term profits over the strategies that used to lead to long-term growth. Wall Street's demand for short-term profits forced most corporations to slim down their organizations and eliminate the functions that did not show a quick ROI.

---

[1] G. Mukunda. June 2014. *The Price of Wall Street's Power*, Harvard Business Review.
[2] R. Foroohar. 2016. *Makers and Takers* (New York, NY: Crown Business).

The growth of financialization also begs another important question. If innovation is the strategy that will keep America in the race and its position as global leader, how can it happen without long-term financial support and investment in manufacturing? This is a very strategic question because 70 percent of all private innovation comes from the research and development and new technologies created by manufacturing.

At this point, Wall Street has the upper hand and continues to focus on short-term profits rather than investing in manufacturing or the long term. It is hard to see how American manufacturing will be able to compete with the rest of the world like we did in the 20th century?

Wall Street, particularly big banks and finance companies, have grown in terms of wealth and power as deregulation of New Deal laws progressed. Wall Street took advantage of their freedom from regulation and have abused the privilege. Deregulating the airlines might have been a good idea, but deregulating the financial industry has been a disaster. Here are some examples of their transgressions in their relentless pursuit of short-term profits in the last 40 years:

- *Private equity and corporate raiding*: Corporate raiders contributed to inequality as they dismembered firms, laid off workers, auctioned off the assets, and destroyed entire communities to reap huge rewards for a few stakeholders. The corporate raider approach to making huge returns in a short period of time was very popular with the wealthy and was viewed as necessary part of Free Market Capitalism (FMC); the elimination of the weak. However, some economists believe that every point gained in financialization leads to deeper inequality, slower growth, and higher unemployment.
- *Credit:* As regulations slowly collapsed along with oversight of consumer and mortgage lending, Wall Street introduced predatory lending in the form of high interest rate credit cards with fees and penalties, pay day loans, and subprime mortgages. The predatory lending practices "preyed on the poor and made them poorer."
- *Housing bubble:* The big banks accepted bad mortgages and packaged them as toxic securities to be sold all over the world.

The bubble bursting forced the economy off the cliff and into the Great Recession but nobody went to jail, the shareholders paid the government fines, and the taxpayers were forced to bail them out.

- *Money laundering:* It has been proven that the American Division of the HSBC bank did money laundering for Mexican drug cartels to the tune of $881 billion according to the Justice Department. The penalty to this bank for blatant corruption was a $1.9 billion fine, and the *New York Times* laments that HSBC was too big to indict.

- *Selling short:* Both JP Morgan Chase and Goldman Sachs worked with hedge funds to bet against the toxic mortgages after the crash had started in 2008. They made money by selling short on the financial catastrophe they had created. JP Morgan was fined $296.9 million and Goldman Sachs was fined $550 million for their actions.

- *Insider trading:* The jailed billionaire Raj Rajaraman made nearly $1 million a minute by getting inside information from Goldman Sachs. Wall Street seems to breed people who want to make a fast buck on insider trading. A good example is Stephen Cohen, whose hedge fund, SAC Capital Advisors, was found guilty of insider trading in 2014 and agreed to pay a record $1.8 billion fine. In all of these cases the cheaters are only fined. With few exception nobody goes to jail.

When you examine past efforts to cheat and not play by the rules, I think it becomes obvious that we must do something to curb the enormous power of Wall Street. The operating principles of the big banks became a cesspool of greed and criminal intent, and they give a very bad name to FMC. During the housing bubble, Wall Street was considered the heart and soul of capitalism, but when they were in danger of total collapse, they became socialists, begging the government and tax payers to bail them out.

Why didn't we just let them fail? The answer was that they were "too big to fail." Allowing them to fail could have created a worldwide depression. In fact, in a meeting with Congress on September 18th, 2008,

Treasury Secretary Paulson told the members that $5.5 trillion in wealth could disappear by 2 p.m. of that day. When testifying before Congress after the 2008 crash, Attorney General Erick Holder was asked why he didn't prosecute some of the banks. He answered, "because they were so large that charging them could hurt the economy." So, if we can't let them fail because they will cause so much financial harm to the world, then it becomes obvious that they should have been regulated so they couldn't put the economies of all nations in peril in the first place.

The Power of Wall Street

Controlling Public Company Boards

The financial sector's influence is now so strong that MNCs such as Boeing, Timken, DuPont, Sara Lee, and United Technologies Corporation (UTC) cower under the pressure of cost reduction, short-term profits, and stock prices. The pressure Wall Street exerts on nonfinancial corporations is called RONA (return on net assets). It is the pressure used by Wall Street to judge managers of publicly held corporations to get better and quicker returns to the shareholders.

Players in the financial industry, particularly hedge funds, have amassed enough stock to gain spots on corporate boards and force short-term strategies. A good example is DuPont Chemical. A hedge fund called Trian Fund Management purchased enough DuPont stock to become its fifth-largest shareholder. Trian said publicly it wanted DuPont to double its share price and cut $4 billion from its business. DuPont submitted, cutting 5,000 people from their workforce, including 1,700 from their R&D lab. DuPont's share price climbed 210 percent between 2009 and 2015.

Carl Icahn did the same thing to both Apple and Xerox because he wanted them to return more cash to shareholders. Activity by these hedge funds and other short-term activists have skyrocketed in public corporations. The Harvard Law School Forum on Corporate Governance said board activism is expected to grow and "private equity is sitting on an estimated $1.5 trillion of 'dry powder' for future market activity."

Stock Buybacks

The primary strategy pushed by Wall Street today for quick profits is called stock buybacks. Before 1982, this technique was illegal because of New Deal laws and because it was thought to be a form of stock market manipulation. But in 1982, stock buybacks were essentially legalized by the SEC. When companies buyback their stock, they must pay above current market prices, or no one will sell. This drives the company's stock price up, no matter how good or bad the company is doing.

Stock buybacks became the fastest way to increase wealth, and now companies borrow money to do it. According to Market Watch, stock buybacks totaled $5.3 trillion in the last decade.[3]

In 2016, United Technologies UTC announced it was closing the Carrier air conditioner plant in Indiana, laying off 2,200 employees. UTC said publicly that the reason was that the labor costs in Mexico would save a lot of money. However, the Carrier plant was one of the most profitable plants in UTC. At the same time, after pressure from 50 hedge funds and private equity investor firms, UTC announced to shareholders a $6 billion stock buyback. Many people believe that closing the Carrier plants was a way to help finance the stock buyback and drive up the stock price.

In 2010, former IBM CEO Sam Palmisano set a course designed to deliver $20 earnings per share by 2015. The plan, called the "2015 Road Map," called for a shift to faster-growing businesses, increased productivity, and dividend share repurchase. Later, IBM CEO Virginia Rometty, who replaced Palmisano in 2012, pledged to follow the plan and continue share repurchases. The plan resulted in hundreds of thousands of layoffs.

To help finance this share-buying spree, IBM loaded up on debt. "While the company spent $138 billion on its shares and dividend payments, it spent just $59 billion on its own business through capital expenditures and $32 billion on acquisitions," IBM is only one example of many MNCs who are dependent to satisfy shareholders, rather than building its own business.

---

[3] C. Lanane. July 30, 2020. American corporations have invested $5.3 trillion in stock buybacks in the last decade, Market Watch.

The Timken Company was forced to split into two companies: one making steel and the other making bearings. According to an article in the *New York Times*, the new bearing company then slashed its pension fund contributions to near zero and cut capital investment in half. At the same time, it has quadrupled its share of cash going to stock share buybacks.

In his book *Bad Money*, Kevin Phillips says that starting with the Clinton Administration both Clinton and his Treasury Secretary Robert Rubin saw

> finance leading the nation into a postindustrial era in which services, especially the lucrative financial ones, would replace manufacturing just as the latter had ushered out a shrinking agricultural sector. Finance was the next great elevator ascending into the luminous temple of progress.

I would add that all administrations since Clinton have abandoned manufacturing and focused on supporting the transition to the service economy led by finance. Government has bet all their chips on finance rather than making things.

The problem that government has ignored is that Wall Street is no longer interested in financing of long-term real investment, particularly the investment in capital projects and R&D in the manufacturing industries. Investment in financial assets is crowding out investment in real assets because the pressure is for quick returns and stock buybacks.

Perhaps, the most important point of Kevin Phillip's book is that he makes a good argument that, historically, every country including Spain in the 17th century, Holland in the 18th century, and Britain in the 19th century that turned to finance as their primary industry never had a manufacturing renaissance and became second rate powers.

The real secret to Wall Street's power is investing in lobbying to continue to change the rules and laws of the financialization game to suit themselves. They always seem to be one step ahead of all other corporations and the government because they spend a lot of time and money lobbying Congress and changing the rules and laws to maintain their power. From 2000 to 2020 according to the Center for Responsive

Politics, the finance, insurance, and real estate industries spent $8.8 billion in lobbying Congress and the White House.[4]

Another problem is that Wall Street seems to be intertwined with the very agencies that are supposed regulate it. In the last 40 years, most of the people picked by various presidents to be economic advisers or treasury secretaries always seem to come from Wall Street. People like Timothy Geithner, Robert Rubin, Jack Lew, John Snow, and Hank Paulson who spent most of their careers working on Wall Street or for the Federal Reserve. They all came into government with the financial view of Wall Street based on short-term profits and a strong dollar, rather than what is good for the country or the economy. The problem is that administrations listen to people from Wall Street rather than from main street. Any solution that might upset making money with money like stopping currency manipulation, revaluing the dollar, or reducing the trade deficit are always opposed by ex-Wall Street executives.

The Essence of the Struggle

This has put nonfinancial corporations on the horns of a dilemma, and they must decide whether they should continue to give in to Wall Street on their demand for fast returns or make long-term investments that benefit employees and all of their other stakeholders. The struggle is between activist shareholders who want to force the corporations into short-term profits for the shareholders versus the people who want to manage the corporations for the long-term benefit of society and the economy.

This shift by the corporations away from satisfying all stakeholders and focusing only on shareholders and stock prices for short-term results is driven by Wall Street. The current financial philosophy of Wall Street is extractive not productive. Andy Grove from Intel said "We are not producing wealth by producing goods; we are producing wealth by financial engineering, and the result is a high-profit, low prosperity nation."

In retrospect, deregulating the finance sector was a big mistake and financialization has become a drag on the rest of the economy and the

---

[4] Lobbying by Top Finance/Insurance/Real Estate Industries, Lobbying total 1998–2021, Open Secrets. 2021.

main driver of inequality. But it depends on where you are coming from. If you are a citizen with all of your 401k in the stock market, or a teacher's union that needs to get a good return to support retirement, or a company who depends on imports, or the traditional economist who totally believes in free trade, you probably want to maintain the status quo and leave Wall Street alone.

But if you are part of main street and worried about your future, or a MNC worried about activist board members, then you probably want to reduce the power of Wall Street. The American economy has endured slow GDP growth, wage stagnation, rising inequality, and reduced capital investment as Wall Street has experienced fantastic growth and power. The power of Wall Street must be reduced. When it comes to short-term profits, they simply can't help themselves and will use every tool in their financial engineering toolbox unless they are better regulated.

Perhaps, Wall Street is a good example of FMC at its best. But its lust for short-term profits has the power to push the economy off the cliff again and destroy the manufacturing sector. It is said that these types of capitalists who continually push the legal boundaries would sell you the rope at their own hanging. The one thing that they have proved over the last four decades is that they must be regulated better.

Upton Sinclair remarked, "It is difficult to get a man to understand something when his salary depends on not understanding it." So, one answer is to change the rules so his salary doesn't depend on it.

The primary goal should be to force financialization and the captains of the financial industry back to their original role of being servants of business rather than masters of business. If you are a manager in one of the many nonfinancial corporations, you may want to consider supporting the following solutions:

1. The first thing that needs to be done is the solution proposed by the Federal Reserve Board of Dallas. They said, "The nation's largest banks are a perversion of capitalism and a clear and present danger to the U.S. economy". The report goes on to say that the five largest banks—JP Morgan, Citigroup, Bank of America, Wells Fargo, and U.S. Bancorp—hold 52 percent of all U.S. deposits and are an oligopoly that should be broken up. Sherrod Brown a Democrat sen-

ator from Ohio submitted a bill to break up the big banks but only got 33 votes in the senate.

2. Reduce debt and increase equity: "The more indebted a company is the more they are subject to the whims of the market."[5] Interest payments are tax deductible, so removing the deduction will reduce the power of Wall Street over American Corporations.

3. Some form of the Glass–Steagall Act should be put in place that separates the commercial part of the banks from the investment part. In addition, the FDIC insurance should apply and protect only commercial bank operations not the gambling part of the banks.

4. We should also consider placing a financial transaction tax on all risky transactions like derivatives, credit default swaps, hedge funds, options, futures, and other bank speculation that leads to windfall profits (see Chapter 19). Wall Street may ignore most regulations, but they understand losing some of their profits through a tax. In this case, Wall Street would have to share some of their money with Main Street.

5. Another suggestion is to raise taxes on hedge funds from 15 to 35 percent. Hedge funds profit from insider tips, high-frequency trading, rumor mongering, front-running trades, special tax loopholes, and even from stocks that are failing. Senator Kyrsten Sinema put in August of 2022 forced Democrats to abandon a tax increase on hedge fund managers and private equity wizards as part of the "Inflation Reduction Act".

6. We also need to pass a law that ensures that taxpayers do not have to bail out banks after they fail from speculation. The Dodd/Frank legislation was simply not enough to stop them from repeating their past crimes and the big banks are still too big to fail.

7. We can also offer lower taxes on assets that are kept for the long term and raise taxes on assets sold in the short term.

8. And, of course, we must make derivatives illegal again.

9. Hire treasury secretaries and directors of other regulating agencies from industry not from Wall Street.

---

[5] G. Mukunda. June 20, 2014. "The Price of Wall Street's Power."

10. But perhaps, the best solution is to make the CEOs and top managers of the banks criminally liable for breaking the laws and regulations so that they fear going to jail. These people are not afraid to do it again, so if you can't put some real fear in their heads, they will do it again.

11. The Volcker Rule prohibits banks from using their own accounts for short-term proprietary trading of securities, derivatives, and commodity futures, as well as options on any of these instruments. However, on June 25, 2020, FDIC officials said the agency will loosen the restrictions of the Volcker Rule, allowing banks to more easily make large investments into venture capital and similar funds.[6] The Volker Rule and other parts of the Dodd–Frank legislation need to be aggressively enforced.

The finance industry muscled past manufacturing to become the largest sector of the U.S. economy, and the problem today is that Wall Street is no longer interested in financing of long-term real investment, particularly the investment in capital projects and R&D in the manufacturing industries. Investment in financial assets is crowding out investment in real assets because the pressure is for quick returns and stock buybacks.

The success of the finance industry is based on growing indebtedness and the use of financial engineering tools that redistributes wealth rather than creating new wealth. America is now a debtor nation with a huge current account deficit, $54 trillion of debt, and a huge importer of foreign products.

I think Wall Street is a house of cards that will crash again unless enough regulations can be introduced to change the game. America needs to change the rules of the financial game and get back to real investment that leads to long-term growth and more productive enterprises. Left to their short-term profit strategies, inequality will worsen, manufacturing will not grow, GDP growth will remain low, and the potential for financial crashes will be high.

---

[6] Y. Onaran. August 20, 2019. *The Volcker rule finally gets revised, but Wall Street is different now*, LA Times.

CHAPTER 9

The Problems of Tax Reduction

In the 1980s, Congressional Republicans led an organized effort to get tax cuts through the Congress that were sold as tax cuts for everybody. But to the disappointment of the middle class, when the smoke cleared, most of the money went to the wealthy. One of the chief strategies used to convince the voters that tax reduction was good for everyone was "trickle-down economics" which theorized that the reduction of taxes on the wealthy would create more jobs and increased wages. Instead, it has led to inequality.

The Six Tax Laws

In the 1980s, Congressional Republicans organized an effort to get tax cuts through the Congress that was sold as tax cuts for everybody. But it wasn't just a wealth transfer; people didn't realize that during a time of deficit spending we increased the federal deficit without having the revenue to cover the additional costs.

1981—Economic Recovery and Tax Act: This bill was sold to the citizens as a recovery bill during the recession of 1981 to 1983 that would create jobs. This was the beginning of what would become supply side economics which was based on the assumption that tax cuts would somehow lead to jobs and growth.

The bill reduced the highest rate of taxation from 70 to 50 percent overnight and included an across the board decrease in marginal income tax rates by 23 percent. It also gave big businesses very generous depreciation rates, and it vastly expanded corporate tax loopholes which lowered taxes for corporations by $150 billion over five years.

1986—Tax Reform Act of 1986: A second tax act was passed which was supposedly designed to simplify the tax code, broaden the tax base, and eliminate many tax shelters. Senator Portman (R-Ohio) called on Congress to pass comprehensive tax reform to boost the economy. He refers to Reagan Administration tax cuts that "boosted American businesses by allowing them to compete on a level playing field and eased the financial burden of families."

The reality was the 1986 Tax Act lowered the top tax rate from 50 to 28 percent, while the bottom rate was raised from 11 to 15 percent. Some middle-class citizens got a few bucks in the first years, but the vast majority of the money went to the top 10 percent. The low-class citizens were not represented in this Act and subsequently lost while the rich had a huge victory.

As a result of the 1981 and 1986 bills, the top income tax rate was slashed from 70 to 28 percent. Reagan focused his efforts on slashing taxes but paid little attention to the federal deficits. Reagan's budgets tripled the national debt from $998 billion at the end of Carter's last budget to $2.9 trillion at the end of Reagan's last budget.

The problem was that the 1981 and 1986 tax cuts proved that cutting taxes when there is no offset and during times of deficits increases the deficit and creates serious problems for the country and the economy.

2001—Economic Growth and Tax Relief Reconciliation Act of 2001 (EGTRRA): Even though the country was sinking into a recession and deficits, it did not dissuade Republicans from pushing through more unbudgeted tax cuts. This tax cut was also sold to the citizens using supply side economics that promised jobs for tax breaks.

In the fine print of the bill was also included more itemized deductions for the wealthy as well as steep cuts in capital gains and dividend taxes. By employing "phase-ins," it appeared that the average citizen would get proportionate cuts for ten years. But, instead, the average citizen would get a one-time $300 tax rebate, and as the phased in tax cuts grew through the decade, the top 1 percent of tax payers received a 51 percent tax cut.

2003—Jobs and Growth Tax Relief and Reconciliation Act: This bill was the second tax cut in the Bush Jr. administration and further lowered marginal tax rates—supposedly for all citizens. Since both the 2001 and 2003 bills were passed, the issue of who were the beneficiaries is still hotly debated. The Center on Budget and Policy Priorities concluded that "the largest benefits accrue to the highest income households."[1] President George W. Bush's 2001 cuts were followed by continued job losses for about a year because of the recession, and it wasn't until after 2003 that jobs were created.

The Bush forecast of jobs created by these tax cuts was 3.31 million jobs, but during his eight-year presidency, only 1.08 million jobs were created. The Clinton administration in the decade before Bush created 22.7 million jobs—without tax cuts.

The best analysis of the two Bush tax cuts was by the Center on Budget and Policy Priorities in 2008.[2] They found the following myths and subsequent realities.

1. Tax cuts "pay for themselves."
   A study by the Treasury Department found that cutting taxes decreased revenues.
2. The economy grew strongly because of tax cuts.
   The 2001 to 2007 economic expansion was subpar overall.
3. Extending the tax cuts is important for the economy's long-run growth.
   Extending the tax cuts without paying for them will reduce economic growth.
4. The tax cuts made the system more progressive.
   The tax cuts led to more inequality.
5. The tax cuts made the tax system fairer to small businesses.
6. They provided large gains for those with high incomes and little benefit to others.

A *New York Times* editorial in 2011 said quite clearly, "The full Bush era tax cuts were the single biggest contributor to the deficit over the

---

[1] J. Friedman and I. Shapiro. July 01, 2010. "Tax Returns: A comprehensive Assessment of the Bush Administration's Record on Cutting Taxes, *CBBP*.

[2] Tax cuts: Myths and Realities. May 09, 2008. Center on Budget and Policy Priorities.

past decade, reducing revenues by about $1.8 trillion between 2002 and 2009."[3]

2004: Another example is the special tax break President George Bush gave to large, public corporations in 2004 to repatriate $1 trillion stashed in overseas tax havens to avoid U.S. corporate taxes. He gave them a one-time tax deal of 5 percent taxes under the banner of creating more jobs and investment. Michael Mundaca, Assistant Secretary for Tax policy wrote, "Unfortunately, there is no evidence that it increased U.S. investment or jobs, and it cost tax payers billions."

2017—The Tax Cut and Jobs Act (TCJA): The Tax Cuts and Jobs Act (TCJA) of 2017 was the fifth big tax cut since 1981, reducing corporate taxes from 35 to 21 percent, or by $1.5 trillion over 10 years. I think it is fair to say that the TCJA is the ultimate test of supply side economic theory because just like the previous four tax cuts it promised to create millions of jobs.

Treasury Secretary Steve Mnuchin said in October 2017 that tax cuts would push "GDP growth over 3 percent or higher leading to millions and millions of jobs." Perhaps, the biggest blunder of the Trump administration was the claim that the TCJA "would add $1.8 trillion in new revenue that would more than pay for the $1.5 trillion cost of the tax cuts themselves." The implication is that increased economic growth would boost tax revenues enough to offset the tax cuts. But this optimistic scenario simply did not happen.

To prove that the TCJA worked as proposed requires real investment. The Economic Policy Institute says, "If the TCJA's corporate rate cuts are to even have a chance at reaching your paycheck, first investment has to boom. The results have been abysmal for the TCJA." The data in Figure 9.1 provides no evidence for an investment boom from the TCJA year-over-year change in real, nonresidential fixed investment, from 2005 to 2019.

Figure 9.1 shows that "year-over-year real, nonresidential fixed investment growth continues to stagnate. If the TCJA was working, we should have seen an investment boom. Instead, after the passage of the TCJA,

[3] Taxes the Deficit and the Economy. September 21, 2011. *New York Times.*

Real nonresidential fixed investment

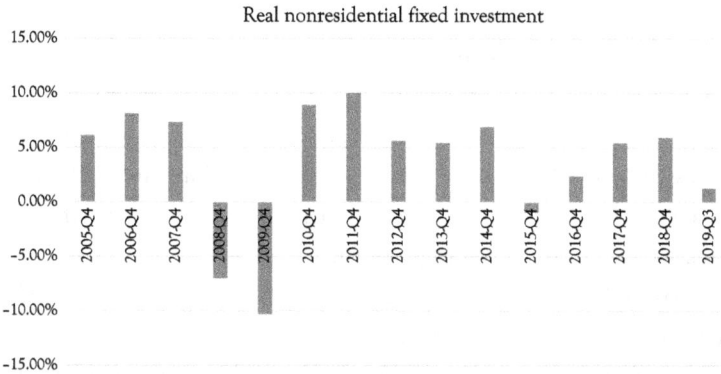

Figure 9.1 Nonresidential fixed investment

Source: EPI analysis of data from table 1.1.6 from the National Income and Product Accounts (NIPA) from the Bureau of Economic Analysis (BEA).

investment growth continued along its pre-TCJA trend for a couple quarters before falling all the way to 1.3 percent in 2019 Q3."

Contrary to the Trump administration claims, the TCJA did not increase GDP over 3 percent, create millions of jobs, or add $1.8 trillion in new revenue that would than pay for the $1.5 trillion cost of the tax cuts; because tax receipts declined and growth did not pay for the tax cuts, the TCJA is simply increasing the federal deficit.

The fact is, prior to the TCJA, few corporations paid the 35 percent corporate tax. After the many deductions offered, 400 of America's largest corporations paid an average federal tax rate of about *11 percent* on their profits in 2019, roughly half the official rate established under President Trump's 2017 tax law, according to *The Washington Post*.[4]

A 2017 study by the Institute for Policy Studies found that across-the-board corporate tax cuts don't do much to create jobs. It compared 92 publicly held corporations who paid less than the 35 percent corporate tax rate. It found that, between 2008 and 2016, these corporations lost jobs while the overall economy increased jobs by 6 percent. Instead of paying taxes or hiring, these companies bought back their own stocks.[5]

---

[4] J. Stein, and C. Ingraham. December16, 2019. *Corporations Paid 11.3 Percent Tax Rate Last Year After Steep Drop Under Trump's Law.*

[5] K. Amadeo. October 30, 2021. "Do Tax Cuts Create Jobs, If so, How?" *The Balance.*

The study also found that what does create jobs is extending unemployment and cutting payroll taxes.

CARES ACT: The Coronavirus Aid, Relief, and Economic Security Act, also known as the CARES Act, was a $2.2 trillion economic stimulus bill passed by the 116th U.S. Congress and signed into law by President Donald Trump on March 27, 2020. This was the 6th tax act that was passed without raising taxes to pay for it.

Overseas Tax Havens: Another tax avoidance scheme used by the U.S. MNCs is to keep their money in overseas accounts (tax havens) rather than bringing them into the United States. In 2017, according to The Institute on Taxation, the 500 largest American companies held more than $2.5 trillion in accumulated profits offshore to avoid U.S. taxes and would collectively owe an estimated $767 billion in U.S. taxes if they repatriated the funds.[6]

They lobbied Congress and the administration to give them a one-time corporate tax holiday at an income tax rate of 5 percent to bring the money into the country. Backers say that it will create thousands of new jobs and new investments, but the last time President Bush gave them a tax holiday in 2004, there was no evidence of new jobs and almost all of the money went to the shareholders.

Tax deductions for outsourcing jobs: In an incredible twist of fate, MNCs are able to get tax deductions when they close American factories and move them to foreign countries. This has been going on since outsourcing began, but it was one of those dirty little secrets not known by the public. A bill to eliminate these tax breaks called the "No Tax Breaks for Outsourcing Act" was introduced in the Congress in March 2021. It would remove incentives for companies to take their business abroad and close the corporate inversion loophole. As of August 2022 Congress hadn't passed this bill.

Tax inversions: Another clever tax avoidance scheme was created by large pharmaceutical manufacturers. They buy or merge with a foreign company and move their headquarters to a foreign country like Ireland—which has a corporate tax rate of 12.5 percent. Many experts agree the

---

[6] Fortune 500 Companies Hold a Record $2.6 Trillion Offshore. March 28, 2017. *Institute on Taxation and Economic Policy, Washington, DC.*

only way to stem the tide of companies moving overseas would be to switch to a more equitable "territorial" system, which would tax corporations only on the income they earn in the United States. Most countries follow the territorial model.

The anti-inversion proposal, announced by the Treasury Department as part of a more detailed version of Biden's new tax plan, would tighten the threshold at which companies lose the tax benefits of doing an inversion.

All of these tax avoidance schemes make me wonder how much tax reduction is enough? Corporations and the wealthiest American have had fantastic increase in total wealth over the last 42 years. Figure 9.2 shows that the gap between federal revenues and outlays continues to widen. Cutting federal deficits during a pandemic is politically impractical, but the logical conclusion is that taxes must be increased or economic problems will become dire.

Most of the gains for the middle class from the New Deal have gone away, and the top 1 percent of income earners have gone from 8 percent in 1978 to 37 percent of the total income of the country (See Figure 1.2 in Chapter 1).

According to the Institute for Taxation and Economic Policy in 2020, 55 American corporations paid 0 taxes, and in fact, they received a

Federal outlays and revenues, 1980-2013
(percentage of gross domestic product)

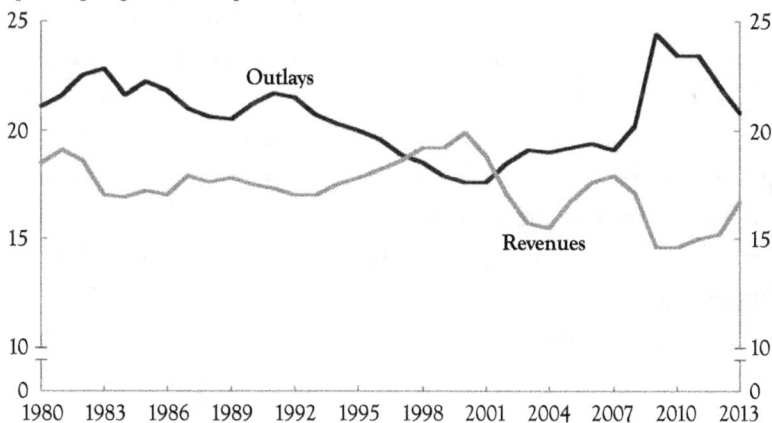

Figure 9.2 Federal outlays and revenues

Source: Summary of receipts, outlays, and surpluses or deficits in current dollars and a percentage of GDP: 1980 to 2013, White House, Office of Management and Budget, Historical tables, Table 1.3, June 7, 2021.

combined federal rebate of more than $3 billion for an effective tax rate of approximately a negative 9 percent. These corporations have lobbied hard for tax deductions such as tax breaks for stock options, credits for research and experimentation, and write-offs for renewable energy and capital investments. President Biden wants to change this and publicly said, "We are asking corporate America to pay their fair share."

The Big Lie—Trickle-Down Economics

There has been a widely accepted economic concept that was created during the Reagan administration and has been used and abused in every election since 1980. It has been called trickle-down economics, supply side economics, and the Laffer Curve, and it assumes that there should be no or few barriers to the accumulation of wealth, because if the rich do well, benefits will trickle down to everybody else. Since the Laffer Curve days, the theory has expanded to suggest that lower tax rates, estate taxes, and capital gains on high-income people and corporations will benefit everyone by increasing GDP growth, wages, and jobs.

The idea of lower taxes that lead to more jobs became so popular that despite recessions and the decline of median income of the middle class, it is still regarded by conservatives as some kind of absolute truth.

For instance, during the vice-presidential debate in 2012, Congressman Paul Ryan said that "Republicans expect tax cuts to create somewhere between 7 and 12 million jobs, grow the tax and balance the budget." If you take his plan literally, you can assume that cutting taxes for the wealthiest people would actually increase tax revenue for the government. The fact is, we have had five tax laws passed since 1981 that lowered taxes to the wealthy and corporations, and there is very little proof that tax reduction had anything to do with increasing the number of jobs or higher wages.

Even though corporations complain about the corporate tax rate, history shows that the effective corporate tax rate has been steadily declining for decades. Figure 9.3 shows that as a percentage of GDP corporate tax revenues dropped to a new low in 1984 after the first tax cut law and have stayed low ever since.

Corporate tax revenue as a percent GDP

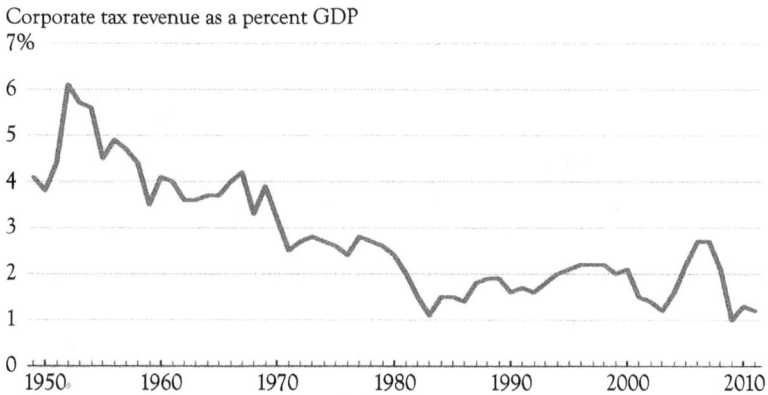

Figure 9.3 Corporate tax revenues are at historic lows
Source: Office of Management and Budget.

The corporate share of total federal tax revenue has dropped by two thirds in the last 60 years. The obvious conclusion is that corporations are simply not paying their fair share.

The Myth That Never Goes Away

The idea that wealthy people and corporations will create more jobs when paying lower tax is a myth that simply won't go away. What the five tax cuts prove is that politicians can make any claim they want about the creation of jobs, growth, wages, and the budget, because they know that once the tax law goes through Congress there will be little, if any, follow-up and the public will lose interest. They now have proved historically that any time they want another tax cut, they only have to bring out another variation of trickle-down economics. It works every time. But in the past 40 years, both government agencies and independent economists have looked into the issue and found there is little or no supporting evidence of a correlation.

In recent years, quantitative studies have been showing up to measure the link between tax reductions, wages, and jobs. The Congressional Research Service (CRS) is a nonpartisan entity associated with the Library of Congress that does academic quality research to answer difficult policy questions.

In 2019, the CRS released a study that concluded that:

> The reduction in top tax rates appears to be uncorrelated with saving, investment, and productivity growth. The top tax rates appear to have little or no relation to the size of the economic pie. However, the top tax rate reductions appear to be associated with the increasing concentration of income at the top of the income distribution. The report notes that tax rates were at the highest when growth was at its peak, and that the reduction in tax rates has not had any discernible impact on the types of investment that lead to growth.[7]

It is also notable that as soon as the CRS report was issued, Senator Chuck Grassley (Republican chairman of the Senate Finance Committee at the time) sent a letter to the CRS taking issue with its findings.

Other studies have also proved that tax rate reductions are correlated with the increasing concentration of income at the top of the income distribution and that supply side theory is flawed. David Stockman, one of the designers of supply side economics, admits that:

> There is no realistic way for "Trickle-Down" economics to work and increase the income of the working classes of America. In fact, I am certain that the developers of the theory of "Trickle-Down" economics were fully aware of this and that "Trickle-Down" has in fact worked as intended. This means that the intent behind implementing "Trickle-Down" was to benefit the wealthiest Americans at the expense of working-class Americans.

Stockman said,

> Giving small tax cuts across the board to all brackets was a "Trojan Horse" that was used to get approval for the huge top bracket cuts. Trickle down was a term used by Republicans that actually meant giving tax cuts to the rich.

---

[7] Professional Staff, Senate Finance Committee. May 31, 2019. *The Economic Effects of the 2017 Tax Revision*, Congressional Research Services Paper R45736.

I was always skeptical of the idea that tax reduction could create jobs, but I also wondered why this idea has pervaded our culture as an acceptable economic theory and had so much traction for so many years. I guess that if you say something often enough and treat it is an absolute economic truth people will accept it. There is now an enormous amount of evidence that proves that increases in jobs, wages, and investment in capital equipment are really driven by demand, not tax cuts, and we need to say this more often.

Politicians need to use this myth to justify selling their programs, and they will continue to use the tax reduction myth and sell it as an economic truth no matter what the evidence.

A good example was Congressman Paul Ryan's Path to Prosperity plan in 2009. He says right in the introduction of his plan that "fixing our broken tax code will create jobs and increase wages." He wanted to reduce taxes in most of the tax brackets, and he also wanted to eliminate capital gains taxes, inheritance taxes, and taxes on interest. He said that "these tax cuts will create nearly 1 million new private-sector jobs next year and result in 2.5 million additional private-sector jobs in the last year of the decade."

He also claimed it spurs economic growth, increasing real GDP by $1.5 trillion over the decade, and it unleashes prosperity and economic security, yielding $1.1 trillion in higher wages and an average $1,000 per year in higher income for each family. However, an analysis of Paul Ryan's tax proposal showed it would give people making around $30,000 per year about $246 per year. But those making more than $1 million a year would save $265,011 per year (according to the Center on Budget and Policy Priorities).

Many supporters of tax cuts are also critics of federal budget deficits, and they don't seem to acknowledge that their tax reduction will increase the deficit (or they don't care). In fact, all tax cuts from now on will increase the federal deficit unless they are passed with offsets.

Figure 9.4 is as chart from the Brookings Institute Hamilton Project which provides context for the debate over tax cuts and tax revenue. It shows that both top income tax rates and corporate tax rates went down below 25 percent during the 1920s. After the crash of 1929, New Deal legislation pushed the top marginal tax rates as high as 90 percent and

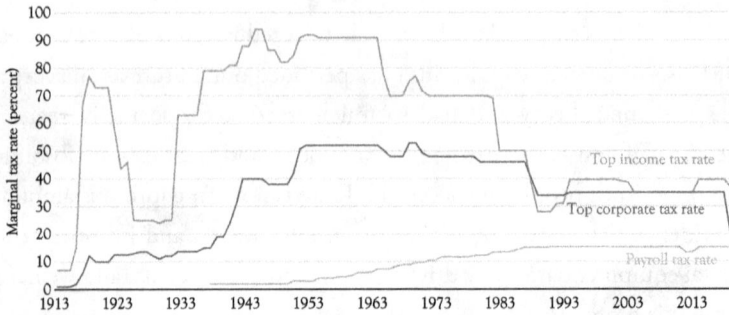

Figure 9.4   Historical tax rates, 1913 to 2013

Source: Internal Revenue Service (IRS) 1913 to 2018; Social Security Administration (SSA) 1937 to 2018; Urban–Brookings Tax Policy Center (TPC) 1913 to 2018; authors' calculations.

Note: Data for the top income tax rates are from the TPC. Data for the top corporate tax rates are from the IRS. Data for the payroll tax rates are from the SSA. Payroll tax includes both the employee and employer contributions.

the corporate tax to 50 percent. It wasn't until the Reagan administration that the top marginal tax rate was dropped from 70 to 35 percent and the corporate tax rate was dropped from 50 to 28 percent. These rates have varied little in the last 36 years and the wealthy have done exceedingly well for four decades. The only serious attempt by the government to find new taxes has been the rise of payroll taxes which was at the expense of working people.

The United States is a relatively lightly taxed economy compared to most Western Nations. High levels of inequality and rising deficits will probably force Congress to consider raising taxes on the wealthy and corporations. The question is whether the multinationals will be willing to "pay their fair share" or do another Dodd–Frank lobbying blitz to keep their taxes down at the expense of the country and maybe the economy? Or they may choose to move their corporations to a low tax country and export their products to the United States.

The specter of multinational corporations (MNCs) avoiding income taxes on billions in profits sends a bad signal to the average American that the tax system is stacked against them. U.S. MNCs have had a good 40-year run of low taxes, and all evidence shows that the tax cuts have not increased jobs or GDP growth. They can help their country and their stakeholders by paying their fair share.

CHAPTER 10

Buying Government With Lobbying Money

Business decided in the late 1970s that if they were going to find ways to increase profits and decrease their costs, they had to buy access to Congress—with lobbying money. Sector by sector, they began to build up large funds to pay lobbyists to get the crucial votes they needed. In 1975, only 175 corporations had lobbyists, but by 2020, they had more than 12,000 lobbyists who were dispensing more than $3 billion per year on lobbying. This new strategy to "buy Congressional Votes" has been spectacularly successful. It would ultimately lower their taxes and get rid of New Deal laws and regulations.

President Reagan campaigned on the notion that *"government is the problem not the solution."* He and the Republican Party characterized government as the boogie man that is the enemy of business and creator of huge deficits. If you listen to big business today, they rant and rave about the sins of big government—particularly taxes and regulations. But I am fond of saying that literally everyone has some part of government they personally like, whether it is the military or the CIA or Social Security or Medicare—there is something for everybody.

In the case of big business, they like—no, love—Congress. Business decided in the late 1970s that if they were going to find ways to increase profits and decrease their costs, they had to buy access to Congress with lobbying money. Sector by sector they began to build up a large fund to pay lobbyists to get the crucial votes they needed. Tom Delay arrogantly called the lobbying effort, "money for access" and that was exactly what it was—money to buy votes from Congress.

This chapter explains how multinationals use their lobbyists and spend millions of dollars influencing legislators to write and maintain laws that suit them. They managed to change or rewrite labor laws that would help them bust unions, negotiate trade agreements that favor the MNCs over labor, give them big tax breaks, and pressure the government to ignore the trade deficit and foreign currency manipulation.

Yes, big business has had a love affair with government for more than 40 years, and it has been wildly successful. Besides improving on the profits of big business, it has also contributed to a massive shift of wealth and rising inequality in America.

Even though lobbyists say they simply want a chance to make their case to government, what they are paying for is making decisions to favor their special cause. I will make the case that special interest groups have the money and the power to purchase congressional votes and that the return on their investment in lobbying is fantastic.

In 2020, lobbyists spent nearly $3.5 billion to influence federal lawmakers according to Open Secrets, driven by an all-out push by most industries to influence the COVID-19 stimulus package. The lobbying system is best described as a "pay to play" system where money buys Congressional and federal agency votes.

Examples of How Lobbying Works

Pharmaceutical industry: It was the pharmaceutical industry that around year 2000 came up with the idea for Medicare Part D, the prescription drug benefit. But, besides the sales of more drugs, the legislation included a provision that forbade bulk purchasing by the government. In 2018, the United States spent an estimated $3.6 trillion, or 17.6 percent of GDP on health care, including $345 billion on prescription drugs. This was $520 per person spent in 1999 and $1,025 per person spent in 2017 on prescription drugs. So, the legislation that forbade bulk purchases was a very big deal and doubled the cost of prescription drugs.

From 1999, all industries spent $64.3 billion in lobbying Congress and federal agencies. The highest investment of all industries was the pharmaceutical industry which spent $4.7 billion followed by the insurance industry which spent $3.2 billion. During this 20-year period, 1,375 organizations in the health care and pharmaceutical reported lobbying expenditures. The efforts were primarily aimed at keeping drug prices high and to not allow Medicare to purchase bulk products to lower the prices, particularly of generic drugs, which are mostly imported from Asia.

The following list is a who's who in the pharmaceutical industry and how much they spent on lobbying (in millions of dollars) according to the Center for Responsive Politics. The list includes Pharmaceutical Research[1] Association $422.3, Pfizer $210.2, Amgen $192.7, Eli Lilly $166.2, Merck $143, Roche $136, Novartis $130.2, J&J $130, Sanoff $116.7, Bayer $111, Glaxo Smith $110.8, Bristol Meyers $101.6, Abbot Labs $96.6, Medtronic $63.8, Baxter Intl. $58.4, Astra Zeneca $54.6, and seven others for a total of $180 million.

Unions: In 1972, a community of CEOs formed the Business Roundtable, a lobbying organization devoted to political influence. The corporations hired lobbyists, and one of the first issues they went after was labor law. In 1978, labor unions decided to make a stand by introducing a bill that would promote union organizing and strengthen the decision making of the National Labor Relations Board (NLRB) by increasing penalties to violators. Business organized against the bill and outspent labor by 3 to 1.

The labor union bill passed the house but was tabled in the Senate and would never return. This was the beginning of a long period of amendments to labor laws, and unions would never recover. Private labor unions declined from 35 percent in 1950 to 6.3 percent in 2020. Today, the corporations out spend unions $34 to $1.[2]

Financial Sector

In October 2010, the DOL proposed a "fiduciary rule" to protect employee retirement accounts from brokers who charge exorbitant fees and put their own commissions above earning returns for their clients. The idea was simple: if you're looking after someone's money, you should look out for their best interests.

---

[1] O.J. Woulters. May 2020. *Lobbying Expenditures and Campaign/Contributions by the Pharmaceutical and Health Product Industry in the U.S., 1999–2018.*

[2] P. Wallach. April 13, 2015. *America's Lobbying Addiction* (Brookings Institute).

It's an obvious rule—but it would cut into financial industry profits, so the industry used its lobbyists to overwhelm Congress with public comments. It worked, and on September 19, 2011, the DOL withdrew the proposed rule.

The Obama DOL proposed the rule again on February 23, 2015. Again, the industry overwhelmed Congress with comments and it took so long that Trump was elected President before the rule could be approved. Trump's Department of Justice refused to defend the rule in court and killed it again. Trump had installed Eugene Scalia as Director of the DOL—the very corporate lawyer and ex-lobbyist who brought the lawsuit to kill off the labor proposal.

Energy Industries

The open secret database shows how the oil and gas industry sowed doubt about climate change from 2005 to 2015. Exxon and other oil companies spent $5 billion during this 10-year period to shape public policy and fight clean energy policies. During that 10-year period, fossil fuel interests outspent renewable energy interests by more than 13 to 1. In the two-year midterm election period of 2017 to 2018, the fossil fuel industry spent $266 million in lobbying and $93 million in campaign contributions to national level candidates, or a total of $500,000 per day.[3]

Koch Industries, Exxon, and Chevron were the top three lobbying spenders, and except for Senator Joe Manchin the money went to 16 Republican Senators. This is incontrovertible proof that the oil, gas, and coal industries do not agree with the threat of climate change, or even if they do agree, they are committed to profit as more important than the threat of climate change.

Lobbying and Federal Contracts

During a four-year (2014 to 2017) period, Fortune 100 companies invested $2 billion in lobbying Capitol Hill and received $3.2 billion in

---

[3] K. Kirk. January 6, 2020. *Fossil Fuel Political Giving Out Distances' Renewables 13 to One, Yale Climate Connections* (Yale Center for Environmental Connections).

Table 10.1 Fortune 100 companies receiving the most federal money

Company	Total federal funding	Contracts	Grants	Lobbying
Lockheed Martin	$137,869,696,565	$137,592,551,097	$277,145,468	$56,610,000
Boeing	$82,088,056,880	$81,314,375,942	$773,680,947	$72,480,000
McKesson	$30,158,912,106	$30,158,749,858	$1,622,481	$3,110,000
General Dynamics	$24,113,132,875	$24,081,664,468	$31,488,407	$43,190,000
Humana	$13,708,974,698	$13,708,874,698	$100,000	$7,655,131
Centene	$13,142,019,332	$13,142,019,332	$?	$9,369,000
United Technologies	$10,698,445,387	$10,635,640,739	$62,800,648	$46,000,000
United Health Group	$10,392,981,044	$10,392,918,093	$62,951	$12,370,000
Honeywell	$8,987,899,368	$8,783,471,110	$204,329,249	$20,460,000
General Electric	$7,131,599,776	$6,979,256,851	$149,160,121	$53,540,000
Totals	$338,291,619,041	$336,795,502,198	$1,498,934,039	$324,775,131

Source: FY2019 data compiled by Open The Books.com via the Freedom of Information Act.

federal grants. The top 10 lobbying companies saw an ROI of 1,000 to 1, or $1 invested in lobbying returned $1,000 in contracts. Table 10.1 from Open Secrets shows how it worked during that period.

55 Corporations Paid 0 Taxes in 2020

It is no coincidence that in 2020, 55 corporations paid $0 federal corporate income taxes and spent $450 million on lobbying, according to a Public Citizen report. Not only were these 55 corporations exempt from paying taxes, but they also received money back from the government through tax rebates. "In addition to the $8.5 billion in tax avoidance, these companies received $3.5 billion in tax rebates."[4]

---

[4] J. Fonger. August 11, 2021. *Corporations Are Spending Millions on Lobbying to Avoid Taxes* (Public Citizen).

The large corporations have the advantage of using the tax code based on 43 tax credits, deferrals, and exceptions. For the most part, these credits and exemptions aren't available to small and midsize businesses who cannot afford to hire DC lobbyists. The essential point is that when large corporations don't pay their fair share, smaller businesses and citizens must pay.

So, despite all those cries and moans about big government, in reality, government has been a very good supporter of big business. In fact, one could make the case that the partnership is a symbiosis of the two. The big corporations used Congress and the democratic processes to get their way and achieve their financial goals.

The list provided in Table 10.2 is notable because all of these companies are either U.S. MNCs or their associations. The U.S. Chamber of Commerce and the Business Roundtable are associations who represent the interests of the multinationals. Companies 3, 4, 5, 6, and 10 represent the health care and pharmaceuticals industries and are mostly concerned with keeping health care prices high. Boeing, Lockheed Martin, Northrop Grumman, and General Electric are part of the aerospace companies shown in Table 10.1 who receive the most federal funding in terms of grants and contracts. AT&T, Comcast, and Verizon control the majority of the telecommunications industries. These 20 corporations account for $7,948,366,258 of the lobbying expenditures since 1998.

The primary problem of lobbying is that lobbyists represent the narrow interests of a specific corporation or industry, and these interests may not align with the country, the economy, or the majority of the citizens. If the multinationals are really serious about leading their companies not just for the benefit of their investors, but "for the benefit of all stakeholders: customers, employees, suppliers, communities, and shareholders; then lobbying is a target rich environment to prove that they can walk their talk."

I see many opportunities for them to prove they are willing to help their employees, customers, and the country. For instance, the fossil fuel industry can prove that they are concerned about the climate crisis by not spending millions of dollars trying to debunk it as an exaggeration. Or the pharmaceutical industry could support Medicare's efforts to buy medicine in bulk, thus lowering drug prices for the Americans who can

Table 10.2 Top 33 lobbying spenders of 2016[5]

Client	2016 Spending	2015 Spending	2015 Rank
1. U.S. Chamber of Commerce	$103,950,000	$84,730,000	1
2. National Association of Realtors	$64,821,111	$37,788,407	2
3. Blue Cross Blue Shield	$25,006,109	$23,702,049	3
4. American Hospital Association	$20,970,809	$20,687,935	7
5. Pharmaceutical Research and Manufacturers of America	$19,730,000	$18,920,000	9
6. American Medical Association	$19,410,000	$21,930,000	4
7. Boeing	$17,020,000	$21,921,000	5
8. National Association of Broadcasters	$16,438,000	$17,400,000	10
9. AT&T	$16,370,000	$16,370,000	13
10. Business Roundtable	$15,700,000	$19,250,000	8
11. Alphabet	$15,430,000	$16,660,000	12
12. Comcast	$14,330,000	$15,680,000	14
13. Southern Co.	$13,900,000	$12,860,000	18
14. Dow Chemical	$13,635,982	$10,820,000	26
15. Lockheed Martin	$13,615,811	$13,954,053	17
16. NCTA—The Internet and Telephone Assoc.	$13,420,000	$14,120,000	16
17. FedEx	$12,541,000	$12,405,835	20
18. Northrop Grumman	$12,050,000	$11,020,000	24
19. Exxon Mobil	$11,840,000	$11,980,000	21
20. Amazon	$11,354,000	$9,435,000	34
21. CTIA	$10,970,000	$10,150,000	29
22. General Dynamics	$10,739,944	$10,259,890	28
23. Verizon Communications	$10,080,000	$11,430,000	23
24. Altria Group	$10,060,000	$9,630,000	32
25. Amgen	$9,860,000	$10,525,000	27
26. Koch Industries	$9,840,000	$10,830,000	25
27. American Bankers Association	$9,831,000	$12,690,000	19
28. Pfizer	$9,750,000	$9,417,650	35

(*Continued*)

---

[5] M.R. Wilson. July 2, 2017. "Lobbying's Top 50: Who's Spending Big, *The Hill.*

Table 10.2 (Cont.)

Client	2016 Spending	2015 Spending	2015 Rank
29. Prudential Financial	$9,400,000	$7,962,500	47
30. Biotechnology Innovation Organization	$9,230,000	$8,350,000	42
31. United Technologies	$9,165,000	$11,470,000	22
32. American Chemistry Council	$9,020,000	$10,050,000	30
33. Royal Dutch Shell	$8,990,000	$8,700,000	37

Source: Data provided to *The Hill* by the Center for Responsive Politics, opens secrets.org.

no longer afford their medicine. Or the hospitals, doctors, and medical associations who protect rising health care costs rather than looking for ways to lower them. Or the telecom giants who have been protecting their monopolies and charging customers twice the rate of the same services as European countries offer.

Senator Elizabeth Warren suggested

A new tax on excessive lobbying that applies to every corporation and trade organization that spends over $500,000 per year lobbying our government. This tax will reduce the incentive for excessive lobbying, and raise money that can be used to fight back against this kind of onslaught when it occurs.

CHAPTER 11

The Rise of Monopolies and Oligopolies

This chapter makes the argument that in the current economy, capitalism is not really promoting the ubiquity of competitive markets; rather, it is quickly moving toward consolidation and oligopolies. The growing influence of oligopolies is a primary driver of inequality and redistribution of income. Consolidation and oligopolies have become the norm and are a dangerous threat to the economy.

Capitalism is a free-market system that is supposed to promote competition. In classic capitalist theory, competition leads to innovation and more affordable prices for consumers. Without competition, a monopoly, oligopoly, or cartel may develop. A monopoly occurs when one firm supplies the total output in the market; the firm can then limit output and raise prices because it has no fear of competition. If several companies get together to control output and prices, it is known as an oligopoly or a cartel.

The political defense of capitalism is that economic power is diffuse and cannot be aggregated in such a manner as to have undue influence over the democratic state. Both of these core claims for capitalism are demolished if monopoly, rather than competition, is the rule. I will make the argument that, in the current economy, capitalism, as led by U.S. Multinational Corporations (MNCs), is not promoting the ubiquity of competitive markets. Rather, it has been moving toward consolidation and oligopolies for many years.

In the last 20 years, oligopolies have been created by mergers and acquisitions (M&A) of MNCs. According to the Coalition for a Prosperous America, "The heated pace of mergers and acquisitions, driven by low global interest rates that makes it cheap for large companies to borrow billions of dollars to acquire other companies." According to a report by financial data firm Refinitiv from October 2021, "Globally, 2021 is the strongest opening nine months of M&A since records began. In the U.S. alone, M&A has surged 139 percent to $2 trillion."

The formation of monopolies and oligopolies also occurred in the Gilded Age, when the robber barons controlled entire industries, including oil, railroads, steel, and the telegraph. The consolidation did not stop until President Theodore Roosevelt broke up the monopolies using antitrust legislation.

A second Gilded Age is happening all over again. We have entirely too many examples.

Modern-Day Oligopolies

1. *Airlines:* In the 1970s, more than 30 major airlines operated in the United States. Some of them had been around a long time, such as Pan American, Trans World Airlines, Eastern, National, United, and Braniff, to name just a few. Through mergers, acquisitions, and bankruptcies, that number was reduced to six major airline companies. In the last decade, as United merged with Continental, and American swallowed U.S. Air, there are now only four major carriers in the United States—United, Delta, American, and Southwest which control 55 percent of revenue—plus 17 minor players. Now all four of the major carriers are profitable, pay dividends, buy back their stock, and control the industry pricing.

2. *Banks*: As everybody now knows, the big banks also have been merging and consolidating. With the repeal of the Glass–Steagall Act in 1999, the big banks refocused their business on proprietary trading—essentially gambling with depositor's money. Today, the big banks contribute more money to proprietary trading then they do to loans to consumers and businesses. The irony is that the big banks are still too big to fail, and they can rely on what has been, to date, the fact that in gambling they know that nobody will go to jail, and the government (and us taxpayers) will bail them out.

   After the big banks collected toxic mortgages and then securitized them to be sold all over the world, the amazing thing was that the government allowed them to use the money to subsidize mergers, such as Wells Fargo's takeover of Wachovia, JPMorgan Chase's acquisition of Washington Mutual, and add to that Bear Sterns and Bank of America's absorption of Countrywide Financial and Merrill Lynch, which accelerated consolidation and created the bank oligopoly we have today. The top five banks in the United States are JPMorgan Chase, Bank of America, Citibank, U.S. Bank, and Wells Fargo, and they control 40 percent of the deposits of the entire banking system.[1]

3. *Hospitals:* In the last 30 years, hospitals in most cities have been merging and consolidating in local markets. Though not national examples, they have formed local monopolies in cities, often leaving only a few hospitals to choose from. These mini-monopolies are also able to boost the prices for most of their services. Hospital pricing is the leading cause of health care cost increases. We've seen price increases of 50 to 100 percent on services from blood tests to chemotherapy. As long as they are allowed to form oligopolies, there is no incentive to focus on the reduction of health care costs.

4. *Meat packers:* In 1982, the five largest meatpackers controlled 16 percent of the meat industry. Today, four firms control 85 percent of the beef market. This is an oligopoly that includes National Beef, Cargill, Tyson, and JBS (which purchased Swift). The big four import much of their meat from Brazil, Mexico, and Australia, which puts enormous pressure on domestic farmers and ranchers who have to pay the price demanded by the oligopoly. Foreign beef is not yet labeled by country of origin, so consumers are not aware that the meat is imported.

5. *Microsoft:* This company has dominated the computer operating system market since the inception of the IBM personal computer in 1981. In 2008, it had 95 percent of the U.S. market. In September 2021, it had 71 percent of the world market. Legal efforts to break its monopoly both in the United States and in Europe have failed.

6. *Beer:* This industry is an almost perfect example of consolidation. Those of us who were of drinking age in the 1970s can remember going

---

[1] Trefis Team, Contributor Forbes Magazine. December 14, 2017. "The Five Largest U.S. Banks Hold More Than 40% of All Deposits," *Forbes Magazine.*

to the supermarket and seeing an entire aisle of domestic beer brands to choose from. At that time, there were 43 firms making beer, and the largest had 25 percent of the market. Today, two firms—Anheuser Busch and Miller/Coors—own 90 percent of the noncraft beer market.

7. *Oil and gas*: There are currently 50 oil and gas producers in the United States producing 2,736 million barrels of oil per year. Exxon merged with Mobil Oil (ExxonMobil) and Conoco merged with Phillips (ConocoPhillips), along with Chevron and Occidental Petroleum. These three giants have 70 percent of all oil produced in the United States.

8. *Technology companies*: Google now owns 92 percent of the Internet search business and Facebook controls 70 percent of social networks. Facebook purchased its two largest competitors Instagram and What's App without any regulatory challenges. According to Market Watch, in the last decade, Google, Amazon, Facebook, and Microsoft have acquired 500 competitors.

9. *Smartphones*: The United States is the second-largest smartphone market after China, with over 260 million users. As of 2020, Apple and Samsung dominate the smartphone market in the United States, with 46 and 25 percent of the market.

10. *Pharmaceutical companies*: The special advantage of pharmaceutical companies is that they are issued patents for new drugs which allows them monopoly pricing for 12 to 13 years. The largest firms then merge or acquire other firms that have patents, which gives them monopoly power in more drug markets. The bottom line is that drug prices in the United States are twice as high as all European drug prices. For instance, the 25 largest pharmaceutical corporations have an average profit margin of 50 percent versus the 25 largest software have an average profit margins of 13.4 percent.

In 1983, Congress passed the Orphan Drug Act (ODA) which governs the approval of drugs for rare diseases. It was supposed to incentivize pharmaceutical innovation via multiple tax breaks and seven years of market exclusivity. There are 7,000 rare disorders affecting 25 to 30 million Americans, and the patients who have these rare diseases live in fear that the pharmaceutical company will raise prices beyond their ability to pay.

THE RISE OF MONOPOLIES AND OLIGOPOLIES   101

A new breed of pharma company has emerged that doesn't invest in research. They buy the companies that have invented the drug and have a patent. The business model is to buy the company and patent, and then to raise prices on the patented drug for a quick profit. A good example is Questor who purchased the rights to Aethr Gel, a drug used to treat a rare form of infantile epilepsy.[2] Questor raised the price of the drug from $40 to $23,000. These exploitive companies will exacerbate the problem of rising health care costs and jeopardize the lives of many patients who cannot afford it.

11. *Railroads*: Since deregulation in 1980, 33 firms have been consolidated into just seven. These Wall Street-owned railroads then cut their workforce by 33 percent over the last six years.

These are not the only examples of oligopolies. Consolidation has occurred in almost every industry and hundreds of market niches.

How Did This Happen?

In the 1960s, Robert Bork was a conservative judge who truly believed socialism might take over the country through the antitrust laws. In 1978, his book, *The Antitrust Paradox,* featured the famous sentence, "The Congress enacted the Sherman Act as a consumer welfare prescription." One year later, the Supreme Court adopted that sentence—which shifted the whole argument away from efforts by corporations to create monopolies and oligopolies to protecting "consumer welfare."

About the same time, economists at the Chicago School of Economics began to publish studies claiming that the enforcement of our anti-monopoly laws was harming that defenseless figure—the American Consumer—by promoting wasteful competitions. The Chicago economists saw monopolies as a move toward efficiencies and that "monopoly was thus naturally fleeting and rapidly turned into competition, so it could be ignored."

---

[2] A. Pollack. December 29, 2012. *Questor Finds Profits, at $28,000 a Vial,* New York Times.

This assumption led to the abandonment of antitrust by the government, which began during President Reagan's term. After he took office in 1981, his new head of the antitrust enforcement, William F. Baxter, swiftly abandoned efforts to promote competition and promised instead a policy based on efficiency considerations. The new focus was on consumer harm with a presumption that the market was naturally competitive, placing the burden of proof on those who thought otherwise. Baxter said the goal was to promote the welfare of the consumer—theoretically by increasing his or her access to cheap goods.

So began the subtle changes using the consumer welfare argument as a cover to justify more consolidation of firms to form monopolies and oligopolies. There was no populist uprising, few protests—virtually nobody challenged the new policy. The free-market capitalists had hit another home run. It gave corporations a free pass to merge and legally form oligopolies and cartels—and the ability to control output and raise prices at the expense of the consumer.

Today, the control of large markets and industries is not an exception, it is the rule. There was no challenge to the abandonment of antitrust from the Reagan and Bush administrations through the Clinton and Obama administrations. Instead of protecting the consumer, oligopolies have exploited the consumer.

Why Increasing Industry Consolidation Matters

Oligopolies and monopolies are the antithesis of how capitalism is supposed to work. Capitalism is based on the ubiquity of competitive markets, but industry after industry is now dominated by oligopolies with few competitors, which leads to an increase in price relative to costs.

Under oligopoly and monopoly conditions, investment slows down. Corporations are better able to raise prices and profits without investing in new technologies and products—declining investment can lead to declining innovation and stagnation.

Industry consolidation controls income redistribution. Oligopoly power can reduce employee wages and benefits, on the one hand, and increase prices, on the other hand. It is the perfect formula for shifting income from the worker to the oligopoly companies.

Oligopolies have the power to reduce supplier prices. As consolidation continues to grow, there are more sellers (suppliers) and fewer buyers (oligopolies), so the buyers gain. For example, a pig farmer today can sell to only four major pork producers. The average price a farmer can get for a hog dropped 31 percent from 1989 to 2008.

Another example, if you are a small manufacturer selling to Walmart, they will pressure you to lower your price by comparing your goods to that produced by its Chinese suppliers. They have 6,000 Asian suppliers and only 1,000 American suppliers.

Consolidation has given many of the large firms the ability to avoid taxation. According to Joseph Stiglitz, "Just 5 American firms, Apple, Microsoft, Google, Cisco, and Oracle, collectively have more than half trillion dollars stashed abroad as they achieve tax rates in some cases well under 1 percent of profits."

The political consequences: The agglomeration of market power also leads to political power where the oligopolies and monopolies create and control the rules of the economic game which leads to political inequality.

I think it is in capitalism's DNA to create oligopolies and monopolies, and they can only be restricted by government regulation. The only answer is antitrust. However, ever since the breakup of AT&T, there have been very few antitrust cases. Regardless of whether Democrats or Republicans are in the White House, the Justice Department has remained inactive in terms of antitrust activity.

Joseph Stiglitz summarizes the problem as,

> We have become a rent-seeking society, dominated by market power of large corporations, unchecked by countervailing powers. And the power of workers has been weakened, if not eviscerated. What is required is a panoply of reforms—rewriting the rules of the American economy to make it more competitive and dynamic, fairer and more equal. Much is at stake—not just the efficiency of our market economy, but the very nature of our democratic society.

Proposed Solutions

Consolidation has not been good for working people, taxpayers, the middle class, and suppliers. People have deluded themselves by thinking that oligopolies are simply the natural outcome of Free Market Capitalism (FMC), globalization, or other mysterious economic forces. It is time to accept the fact that this consolidation contributes to redistribution of income, lower wages, inequality, lower standards of living, and a slow-down in productivity. "In short, the poor performance of the American economy in so many dimensions."[3]

The answer is to revive antitrust as it was used in the New Deal and President Joe Biden started down the antitrust road when he signed an executive order in July 2021 targeting what he labeled as anticompetitive practices in tech, health care, and other parts of the economy, declaring it would fortify an American ideal "that true capitalism depends on fair and open competition."

The sweeping order includes 72 actions and recommendations that would lower prices for families, increase wages for workers, and promote innovation and faster economic growth. Biden said "Let me be clear: Capitalism without competition isn't capitalism."

To begin addressing the trend, the order encourages the Justice Department as well as the Federal Reserve, the Federal Deposit Insurance Corporation, and the Office of the Comptroller of the Currency to update guidelines to provide greater scrutiny of mergers. It also encourages the Consumer Financial Protection Bureau to issue rules allowing customers to download their banking data and take it with them when they switch.

The order includes several provisions that could also affect the agricultural industry. It calls on the U.S. Department of Agriculture to consider issuing new rules defining when meat packers can use "Product of USA" labels. It also encourages the FTC to limit the farm equipment manufacturer's ability to restrict the use of independent repair shops or

---

[3] J. Stiglitz. October 26, 2017. *America Has a Monopoly Problem and It Is Huge* (The Roosevelt Institute).

do-it-yourself repairs—such as when tractor companies block farmers from repairing their own tractors.[4]

In January 2022, the Biden administration pledged $1 billion in rescue funds to small and independent meatpackers to counteract the oligopolies control of the meat packing industry. This provides some relief to the smaller companies in the industry but begs a bigger question. Is the answer to oligopoly and monopoly control of markets and pricing going to be a government bailout in each industry affected, or would a better solution be to implement antitrust laws to break up the oligopolies as happened early in the 20th century and in the Depression? The oligopoly problem is driven and controlled by MNCs, and the only hope for change is by Congress.

Senator Amy Klobuchar, a Minnesota Democrat who chairs the Senate Judiciary Subcommittee on Competition Policy, said that Biden's executive order needs to be buttressed by congressional action. "Competition policy needs new energy and approaches so that we can address America's monopoly problem," Klobuchar said, "That means legislation to update our antitrust laws, but it also means reimagining what the federal government can do to promote competition under our current laws."[5]

---

[4] A. Madhani and M. Gordon. July 9, 2021. "Biden Signs Order Targeting Big Businesses," *U.S. News.*

[5] K. Rapoza. July 29, 2021. "Congress Takes on Beef Monopoly in Dual Hearings," *Coalition for a Prosperous America.*

CHAPTER 12

The Jobs Are There. Where Is the Training?

The manufacturing workforce skills shortage is growing as apprentice-ships and training are declining. There is no evidence that most of America's Multinational Corporations (MNCs) are investing in long-term, high-skill training that would help the skilled worker crisis in America.

A 2018 study by Deloitte and the Manufacturing Institute (MI) predicted that U.S. manufacturing would have 2.1 million unfilled jobs by 2030. In June 2022, the Department of Labor (DOL) Job Openings and Labor Turnover Survey (JOLTS) showed 793,000 unfilled manufacturing jobs. I tried to find out how many of these unfilled jobs are skilled versus unskilled, but nobody I talked to at the DOL had any idea. In fact, I couldn't find anyone in government or industry who had any idea what kinds of manufacturing jobs are going unfilled.

Skilled Worker Shortages Are a Three-Pronged Problem

1. *Entry-level workers*: According to the Deloitte/MI survey, "These are the jobs that do not require technical know-how or industry knowledge, such as team assemblers, production work helpers and hand-held tool cutters and trimmers." They say that manufacturers are willing to pay $15.50 per hour, but that "applications are not pouring in." It is a big problem for manufacturers because new workers without experience can get a job at FED EX as a package handler for $25.50 an hour with an attendance bonus. Wages are going up in many service industries, and $15.50/hour is probably not enough to interest a Starbucks employee to make the switch.

2. *Semiskilled workers*: These are jobs like CNC machine operators, welders, drill press operators, assemblers, grinders, machine operators, and tenders, which require classroom and hands-on training that can take several months up to one year.
3. *Highly skilled jobs*: These are the most critical manufacturing jobs because highly skilled workers are retiring faster than they can be replaced, and many industries need journeyman workers. But advanced training programs such as apprentice training are not growing in the manufacturing sector in the United States.

Training programs that lead to journeyman status take thousands of hours of training, and most of the skills are attained with hands-on learning, not classroom learning. An example is a journeyman machinist, which takes approximately four years or 8,000 hours to attain the 28 skills needed to become a journeyman on a wide variety of manual and CNC machines.

A January 2020 training survey by the MI shows that the average number of hours of training, per employee, among their members (mostly large corporations) is 27.7 hours per year, and for new employees, it was 42.9 hours per year. The training survey also shows that only 32 percent of members have apprentice training programs. MNCs, with a few exceptions, are not investing in advanced training that takes thousands of hours. The study says that "75% of industrial organizations identified reskilling the workforce as important or very important for their success over the next year, but only 10% said they were very ready to address this trend."[1]

The 27.7 hours per year seems to indicate that the MI's members are not going to invest in training the highly skilled employees they need for the future. So, what is their strategy?

Strategies Used for Decades

Instead of investing in long-term training, MNCs have been trying to solve the skilled worker shortage with stopgap measures:

---

[1] G. Carrick, V.P. January 17, 2020. "The Manufacturing Institute Training Survey." www.themanufacturinginstitute.org/wp

- *Hiring H-1B foreign visa workers*: These visas are used mostly for engineers and in the high-tech industries are limited to 85,000 new jobs per year.
- *Outsourcing*: Moving production and jobs to low-cost countries.
- *Automating*: There has been a huge investment in automation such as robots, packaging machines, and automated production lines. But not enough workers can troubleshoot, operate, and maintain the automation, which has added to the skilled-worker shortage problem.
- *Buying services:* There are not enough tool and die and mold-making shops in the United States today. Corporations buy these services from foreign companies.
- *Poaching trained workers*: For many years, corporations have been stealing trained workers from their suppliers by offering higher pay and benefits.

From my interviews with leaders of manufacturing associations, I have concluded that despite the need, most manufacturers, including small and midsize companies, are unwilling to fund long-term training programs and instead want short-term training. The short-term approach will probably work for entry-level workers, but it doesn't answer the multiple skills needed for tool and die, mold making, advanced machining, or all of the maintenance skills needed to troubleshoot, repair, operate, and maintain automated production lines.

The Deloitte report says 2.69 million manufacturing workers will be retiring in the next decade, so more training is probably the only real answer left. The big problem is that skilled people have been retiring for the last decade and are not being replaced. The DOL Statistics in their database showing Private Industry by six-digit NAICS Industry reveals the following:

Machine shops: According to the Bureau of Labor Statistics (DOL), since 2002, the number of machine shops has decreased by 5,295 shops (21 percent) and employment has decreased by 64,342 people (20 percent).

Tool and die makers: Two classes of machinists that are critical to manufacturing are tool and die makers and mold makers. In the United

States however, tool and die makers have declined from 83,463 in 2002 to 55,694 in 2020, a loss of 27,769 workers.

Mold making: Industrial mold companies lost 1,334 shops (45 percent) and 10,481 workers (24 percent) between 2002 and 2020.

Maintenance: The shortages of maintenance workers are most prevalent in the aviation, auto, plastics, and industrial machinery industries. To become a certified maintenance worker takes two to four years of training.

Welders: The American Welding Society says "the industry is predicting a shortage of over 375,000 skilled welding professionals by 2023."

The issue is fourfold. First, the training programs to produce highly skilled workers are few and far between and MNCs are reticent to invest in long-term training. Second, more skilled workers are retiring than are being replaced. Third, young people don't see these highly skilled jobs as a good career investment. Fourth, entry-level pay is not competitive with other industries like Amazon warehouses or FED EX Drivers.

My assumption is that if a good percentage of these jobs are highly skilled, then we will need advanced or long-term training like apprentice training. However, it appears that the manufacturing sector is not investing in apprentice training. I have been following the Office of Apprenticeship training's website since 2001, and the total annual number of registered apprentices in manufacturing has dropped from around 20,950 in 2001 to 15,510 in 2020 (15,510 apprenticeships per year is only 0.0012 percent) of the total manufacturing employees in the United States. Meanwhile, apprenticeships in other sectors such as construction are growing.

Industry Stability

In a November 2, 2021, article in *IndustryWeek* by Paul Wellener, he said that "less than 5 in 10 Americans surveyed believed manufacturing jobs to be as stable and secure as jobs in other industries and less than 3 in 10 Americans surveyed would encourage their children to pursue a manufacturing career." Young people, their parents, and teachers all watch the news and have followed the decades long closing of manufacturing plants and the loss of jobs. They all know that American MNCs reserve the right to outsource production and jobs to low-cost countries around the world and there is little job security. Despite all of the high school workshops and manufacturing day ceremonies, the view of manufacturing is not going to change until the MNCs can address the issues of job security, training, and wages. Here, are some specific recommendations.

- To change the view of manufacturing as an unstable industry is going to require corporations to publicly address the problem of outsourcing and job security.
- They also need to publicly commit to long-term job training and paid internships to replace the highly skilled workers leaving the industry.
- I also think they will have to match the starting wages of Amazon and FedEx to get their fair share of entry workers.

Today, manufacturing can't get entry-level people, the high-skilled people are retiring, and the surveys show there will be 2.1 million jobs unfilled by 2030. If there is going to be a turnaround in American manufacturing, it is going to take a serious investment in advanced training and MNCs are going to have to lead the way.

CHAPTER 13

The Postindustrial Service Economy

It is my contention the "postindustrial" service economy—especially one that that will provide continued economic growth and enough family wage jobs to sustain current living standards—is a myth. The Multinational Corporations (MNCs) have accelerated the problem by outsourcing manufacturing jobs and production to low-cost countries.

In 1973, Daniel Bell wrote a book, *The Coming of Post-Industrial Society*, in which he described how the U.S. economy was transitioning from being manufacturing-based to becoming service-based. He correctly predicted the global diffusion of capital, trade deficits, and the relative decline of the manufacturing sector. Bell also predicted that the importance of blue-collar (manual) work would decline, and that technical and professional work, such as lawyers and computer programmers, would come to predominate. As well, he asserted that theoretical knowledge would become more important than practical know-how and that health, education, and government services would be the most important sectors of the new economy.

Many economists and academics jumped on the "postindustrial" bandwagon and have convinced themselves and most citizens that the transition is a good and inevitable thing. In 2005, *The Economist* published an article that summarizes the prevailing belief about manufacturing employment. The article, titled "Industrial Metamorphosis," carried the following brief description: "Factory jobs are becoming scarce. It's nothing to worry about." The article goes on to say

the issue is not whether people work in factories or not, but whether they are creating wealth. In developed economies today, telecom, software, banking, and so on can create more wealth than making jeans or trainers. Before long no one will much care whether firms are classified under manufacturing or services. Future prosperity will depend not on how economic activity is labeled, but on the economies' ability to innovate and their capacity to adjust.

Michael Boskin, who was economic adviser to George H. Bush said, "It doesn't make any difference whether a country makes computer chips or potato chips." His flippant remark is incorrect, and as it turns out, making chips was not only important for the United States, but the lack of U.S.-made chips has reduced automobile production and has required a federal bailout of the industry to the tune of $52 billion in tax payer dollars.

So, when *The Economist* says there is nothing to worry about, it depends on whether you have a college degree and have a good chance to claw your way into the credentialed elite. But if you are among the 60 percent of workers who have a high-school diploma or less, you may be struggling to make ends meet. Millions of workers in this category feel that something is very wrong in the postindustrial economy and are despondent about their future.

Today, the stock market is near an all-time high, and unemployment is low. In fact, many jobs are going unfilled. So, what is the problem? When you look deeper into the economy, you will find that people cannot find jobs with decent pay and benefits, afford to buy a home, or afford health insurance. They are worried about their future, and their plight doesn't square with the economy described in the headlines.

The big economic question today is can we transition from a manufacturing economy to a service economy and still provide enough good jobs to raise the standard of living for most workers? Contrary to the view of many economists, the smooth transition to the service economy has become a very rough road and has created many losers, and unlike Europe, in America, the government does little to take care of the losers.

I will make the argument that there is growing proof that the postindustrial service economy is not going to provide the wages, living standards needed, or the economic growth in the economy promised by many economists. And that trade policies have led to deindustrialization, slow growth, stagnant wages, lower living standards, and rising trade deficits.

So, What Happened?

Over the last four decades, MNCs decided that it was in the best interest of their shareholders to move jobs and production to low-cost foreign countries. Under the flag of the free market, the public found out that there was no loyalty to the United States. Instead of trying to protect American industries and slow down the rush to low-cost countries, the only real loyalty was to the short-term interests of their shareholders.

Since 1979, America has lost 7.5 million manufacturing jobs (36 percent), and according to the Economic Policy Institute, five million of these jobs were lost since 2001, after China was allowed into the WTO. The reason these jobs are important is that the wages and benefits from manufacturing jobs provided families with a high-school education membership in the middle class. The important point is that lost manufacturing jobs were chiefly replaced by lower wage service jobs.

Outsourcing by American corporations has caused permanent damage to American workers, manufacturers, supplier companies, and the living standards of many families. It may lead to short-term profits for the corporation, but eventually, the corporation will lose the technology and the market to its foreign competitors. Trade agreements such as NAFTA and CAFTA accelerated job losses and along with the China's entrance into the WTO, opened up the flood gates for outsourcing jobs and factories, causing manufacturing to implode, losing millions of "high-quality" jobs.

Will the Service Economy Create Enough Good Jobs?

The real issue that the economists never seem to address is this: What kind of jobs will be created in a "postindustrial" economy? Will there be enough family wage jobs to allow all members of the middle class to raise families? Will the new jobs pay enough to maintain middle-class living standards or to keep the gap between the "haves" and "have-nots" from increasing?

You can find out for yourself by studying the data on the Bureau of Labor Statistics website. Click on the link to "Table 1.4 Occupations with the most job growth, 2020 and projected to 2030 (Numbers in thousands)." Then, add all of the jobs with a median annual wage below $50,000; you will find that in the Bureau of Labor Statistics (BLS) projects, there will be a total of 5,868,700 jobs (65 percent of the total) with an average wage of $39,747 per year. Then, add all of the jobs with a median annual wage above $50,000; you will find that in the BLS projects, there will be a total of 3,242,500 jobs (35 percent of the total) with an average wage of $84,842 per year. With few exceptions, almost all of these higher pay jobs are white-collar jobs that require a college degree or advanced skills.

The job quality index: A new economic indicator called the U.S. Private Sector Job Quality Index (JQI) shows that the economy has produced a lot of jobs, but they are increasingly "low-quality" service jobs. Figure 3.1 in Chapter 3 shows that the quality of new jobs has been decreasing for 30 years. In 2020, the JQI was approximately 81, which means that there are 81 high-quality jobs for every 100 low-quality jobs. This is a significant reduction of good jobs since 1990 when there were 94 high-quality jobs for every 100 low-quality ones.

The Weakening Trend

The reason is obvious. "Lost manufacturing jobs were replaced by lower-wage/lower-hours service jobs. Since 1990, America has cumulatively added some 20 million low-quality jobs, versus around 12 million high-quality ones."[1] In short, the U.S. economy has shifted toward creating more bad jobs than good jobs. This does not bode well for those workers in the middle class with a high-school diploma or less.

According to the Coalition for a Prosperous America,

> historically, there has always been a significant concentration of labor in lower quality jobs. Over the past three decades, however, this concentration has significantly increased moving from a JQI level of 94.9 in 1990 to 81.0 as of July 2020. Put

---

[1] G. Guilford. November 21, 2019. "The Great American Labor Paradox: Plentiful Jobs, Most of Them Bad," Quartz.

differently, low-wage/low-hours jobs constituted 52.7% of total Production and Non-Supervisory positions (P&NS) in 1990, while in the years since they have accounted for 63% of all P&NS jobs created.

Not only has the mix of high- and low-quality P&NS jobs changed in favor of the latter over the past three decades, but the gap in weekly income between the two groups has widened as well.

If a person loses his manufacturing job and has a high-school diploma, he is likely to find a job in one of the following industries:

- Leisure and hospitality industry which has 14.7 million non-management employees earning $16.58 an hour and working an average of 25.8 hours per week.
- Administration and support which has 8.1 million jobs earning an average of $22.36 per hour and working 34 hours a week.
- Retail industry has 13.2 million jobs earning an average of $18.83 per hour and working 31 hours a week.
- Warehousing and transportation which has 5.2 million jobs earning an average of $24.64 per hour and working 38 hours a week.

$25 per hour is only $48,000 per year, so if you are one of the 41 million people who must work in these service industries, attaining the American Dream may be problematic.

The focus by the media and the government has always been to explain the employment story in terms of the total number of jobs available and the unemployment rate. This is an incomplete and often inaccurate description of health of the economy because it refers to quantity not quality of jobs.

The U.S. JQI chart (Figure 3.1) shows the trend toward more low-wage jobs and what is slowly happening to our economy. It is my contention the "postindustrial" service economy—especially one that will provide continued economic growth and enough family wage jobs to sustain current living standards—is a myth.

The best short-term investment opportunity that would create manufacturing and construction jobs, increase tax revenue, and offer a Return on Investment (ROI) is to invest in repairing and replacing America's infrastructure. On November 15, 2021, the President signed into law the Infrastructure Investment and Jobs Act (IIJA), bipartisan legislation which will make available $1.2 trillion in funding for infrastructure programs across the energy, water, transportation, and building sectors. The bill will create 1.5 million jobs per year for 10 years.

What can corporate leaders do now to convince people that they are willing to make some profound changes? Here are some suggestions for positive change that would really help all stakeholders:

1. Reduce outsourcing jobs to low-cost countries. America's biggest corporations continue to outsource jobs and production to low-cost countries. In the past, corporations made the case that outsourcing jobs is a natural function of free-market capitalism (FMC) and is necessary to increase shareholder value. General Motors, Ford, BASF, General Electric, Caterpillar, Chevron, Cisco, Intel, Stanley Works, Merck, United Technologies, Oracle, and many more companies have continued to close plants in the United States and move jobs to foreign countries. But if corporations are really committed to investing in their workers and communities, they could begin by reducing their continued efforts to close plants and eliminate jobs. Providing job security is at the heart of the truth of corporate commitments to their stakeholders.

2. They could also invest more in America and reduce stock buybacks. Stock buybacks are simply a form of stock manipulation to get quick short-term profits and were illegal prior to 1982. Stock buybacks do little to improve business operations and often are made at the expense of long-term capital investment. They are designed solely to benefit shareholders. If corporations are really committed to "serve all stakeholders, not just shareholders," they could prove it by reducing stock buyback commitments.

3. In 2017, 181 CEOs made a public commitment that says that corporations now want to deal "fairly and ethically with our suppliers." They are "dedicated to serving as good partners to other companies

large and small" that help them "meet their mission." If this is true, it would really help American suppliers if corporations would renounce the strategy of taking a supplier's product that is successful in the U.S. market and sending it to Asian companies to copy and produce a lower-cost product.

4. A 2018 survey by the Manufacturing Institute estimates that 3.5 million manufacturing jobs will need to be filled in the next decade and 2.1 million of those jobs will go unfilled. As skilled people have retired, manufacturing companies, particularly MNCs, have not invested in the advanced training programs to replace the retiring workers. This skills gap has been known for 30 years and six major surveys, and there are still not enough advanced training programs to produce the people needed. American corporations could help themselves and their stakeholders by making a public commitment to fund apprentice programs and internships that will train workers up to a journeyman skill level in a variety of different manufacturing locations.

The idea of serving all stakeholders, not just shareholders, is timely and badly needed. The suggestions listed in this chapter are all positive steps that could help American corporations and CEOs realize their new commitments to all stakeholders. In their own words, they said they want to "improve society and push for a society that serves all Americans." Pursuing these suggestions could really help employees, families, communities, suppliers, and customers. Only time will tell if their commitments are simply a public-relations effort, or if they are serious about benefiting more than just their shareholders.

CHAPTER 14

The Threat of China

America is at a crossroads. We must stop dealing with China as we hope they would be and begin dealing with them as they are. The United States is in a favorable position in the struggle because China needs our consumer markets more than we need theirs. It is not an exaggeration to say we are in the beginning of a cold war with China and must defend ourselves just as we did with the Soviet Union. Accepting the status quo like we did for 20 years is no longer an option. Decoupling from China will be a long, slow, and contentious process, but it is time to face reality and do something for the country, our citizens, and American manufacturing. We need short-term sacrifice to avoid long-term collapse. The future is now.

Do you remember when China was accepted into the World Trade Organization (WTO) in 2001? Presidents Clinton and Bush, as well as many other public policy leaders, predicted that it would improve the U.S.–China trade balance and would encourage China to abandon communism for Free Market Capitalism (FMC), both of which would benefit America. I don't know how they got it so wrong.

Clyde Prestowitz in his book, *The World Turned Upside Down*, says

It is also clear that there is no comfortable middle ground. The more one invests in China, the more one feeds the Chinese Communist Party (CCP)-dominated machine while making oneself hostage to coercion by the Party. It is now self-evident that the United States and the free world cannot continue to drift in this direction.

More importantly, Prestowitz goes on to name the true drivers of our China policy-America's Multinational Corporations (MNCs). He says the President must make clear that the interests of the country and of freedom outweigh those of global corporations and investment bankers, and he must explain that the Cold War with the Soviet Union was just a warm-up game for the main match now coming.[1]

The Economist Magazine, which has been a long-term advocate of free trade, said in March 2018 that the notion of changing China from a communist dictatorship to FMC was a false hope. Elizabeth Economy in her book *The Third Revolution* says that contrary to the wishes of U.S. politicians, China has become less liberal, more centralized, and more authoritarian as it has become richer and more powerful.[2]

The original rationalization for allowing China into the WTO was that it would move China to become a more democratic country with an open market. The policy makers assumed that working interdependently with China would bring greater stability because both countries would be more dependent on each other's fortunes. China would then become cooperative and a more honest trading partner and a reasonable competitor.

But it simply did not happen. Instead of becoming more democratic, China under Chairman Xi has intensified the Communist Party's totalitarian power over its people, and it is now a big threat to Hong Kong, Taiwan, and the Uyghur muslims in Xinjiang Province. Instead of becoming an economic partner, they have become an economic destructor—and a threat to U.S. national security. Instead of competing like the United States and other industrial nations, they have chosen to compete using predatory mercantilism.

A more truthful description of China and the Communist Party's intentions is their policy toward the Uyghur population in Xinjiang Province. They have sentenced hundreds of thousands of Uyghurs (who are Muslim) to open air prisons and reeducation camps. They sterilize many Uyghurs and force them to work construction and in factories without pay—essentially slave labor. On January 6, Congress passed the Uyghur Forced Labor Prevention Act (UFLPA) which prohibits the imports to the

---

[1] C. Prestowitz. 2021. *The World Turned Upside Down, America China, and the Struggle for Global Leadership* (New Haven and ondon: Yale University Press).
[2] Elizabeth Economy. 2018. *The Third Revolution—Xi Jinping and the New Chinese State* (Oxford University Press).

United States of any items mined, produced, or manufactured wholly or in part in the Xinjiang Uyghur Autonomous region. I think this new law shows that the support for China and its mercantilist policies is waning.

The U.S. strategy of forbearance: China continually challenges the United States by ignoring free-market rules and doing whatever it takes to capture market share. Meanwhile, the United States looks the other way when China breaks the rules, thus encouraging them to do it again.

The Bush Jr. administration negotiated with China for two years but never laid out any real targets for China and did little to protect American manufacturing. The Bush administration filed a report in 2006 that cited Chinese barriers to some U.S. exports, failure to protect intellectual property, failure to protect labor rights, and extensive government subsidies of Chinese industries and companies. But then there was no enforcement and nothing happened after the report.

The Obama administration also had many meetings with the China, where they discussed climate change, the South China Sea, United Nations issues, green ports, and illegal trade in animals. But like Bush, Obama never pursued reshoring manufacturing during his entire eight years in office, and he never enforced existing agreements.

Every Congress and administration since President Clinton have ignored China's illegal strategies. Instead of facing up to the problems, the United States has chosen dialog, diplomacy, and collision avoidance over enforcement.

This policy is generally called forbearance, which is "refraining from enforcement of what is due." It is based on the illusion that China would eventually see its interests best fulfilled by following the rules. After 21 years since joining the WTO, forbearance has failed, and China is the winner. It is a rogue nation whose reaction to our diplomacy is to be ever more aggressive because we have avoided enforcement. The United States is like the mouse who has seen the circling hawk shadow. Its strategy is to stay very still in hopes the hawk won't see it.

The limited response to China's aggressive trade policy has many origins. First, MNCs and Wall Street spend a lot of lobbying money on both the Congress and the administration to avoid confrontations with China and to maintain the status quo. Obama's Treasury Secretary, Jacob Lew, said doing anything about currency manipulation "would have the unintentional consequences of stopping global banks from buying bonds to combat weak growth."

Kurt Campbell, who was assistant secretary of state for Obama, argued for a policy of conciliation in order to avoid the trap of two great powers clashing (collision avoidance). Other staff members said that Obama worried that putting any pressure to stop China's cheating would put them on the defensive and could backfire. And of course, every administration is worried that if we upset China, they may quit loaning us the money to finance trade deficits. The policy of forbearance has not worked, and it is ironic that the most ruthless and unlawful are winning over the most lawful and ethical.

Still another argument used by conservatives is that anything we do to stop China from cheating will be viewed by China as protectionism, which could lead to a trade war. I find this kind of thinking laughable. We are already in the trade war, and China is the decisive winner. As it turned out, making a trade agreement with China without enforceable penalties for cheating is a long-term ticket to economic oblivion.

We allowed this to happen: America has been complicit in its own demise by politically ignoring China's unfair and illegal strategies for 20 years. Until Donald Trump countered China by imposing tariffs, both Democratic and Republican politicians did nothing to stop China's illegal and unfair policies. We naively supported our economic philosophy of FMC because of our stateless MNCs who rely on imports, while China pursued mercantilist strategies and played by their own rules.

It was naive of U.S. politicians to think that allowing China into the WTO could change China's outlook or governance. But I think that U.S. politicians are slowly waking up to the reality that China is a totalitarian, monolithic, and nationalistic country controlled by the Chinese Communist Party (CCP). China is not a nation on the road to democracy, and Mao Zedong said, "Communism is not love. Communism is a hammer which we will use to crush the enemy."

They are an amoral government that uses predatory mercantilism in its commercial endeavors, and no agreement or negotiation is going to change this fact. So, the question is when will we wake up to the fact that China is a rogue economic power that will always take advantage of weak nations that won't confront cheaters? Appeasing China has been a failed policy from the start because China only responds to leverage, and the U.S. policy of forbearance and diplomacy has simply made matters worse.

China cheating methods: China's authoritarian government has taken advantage of their competitors by ignoring trade agreements and implementing a comprehensive program to get their hands on foreign technologies using a wide variety of tactics such as:

- *Currency manipulation:* China manipulates its currency to keep the U.S. dollar value high, so that Chinese companies have from 20 to 30 percent cost advantage. This undervaluation is illegal and should be considered a direct export subsidy, yet the Treasury Department has refused to treat currency undervaluation as actionable under the law.

- *State-owned enterprises (SOE):* China owns and subsidizes many companies, and it uses these subsidized companies to target a market, capture market share, and drive competitors out of business.

- *Subsidies:* An example is the wind turbine industry, where the Chinese government offers 40 different types of subsidy programs to their wind turbine manufacturers. China's wind turbine company Goldwind is now the Number 3 turbine manufacturer in the world and wants to overtake G.E. and Vestas to be number 1. In 2019, Xiaoguang, a G.E. employee in New York, and a Zhaoxi Zang in China were indicted on charges of economic espionage and conspiracy to steal G.E. trade secrets in turbine technologies, so regardless of the indictment, they probably already have the secrets in China.

- *Technology transfer:* As a condition of accessing the Chinese markets, China requires U.S. companies that build plants in China to create joint ventures with local companies—and share with them their latest technologies. This is a way for China to get our technologies without having to do the R&D.

- *Technology theft:* China knows that technology and innovation is what can make them the Number 1 economy in the world, and they are prepared to get it any way they can.

- *Advanced technology products:* They are particularly interested in getting our advanced technology products all of which are central to U.S.'s own innovation strategy. In 2020, the U.S. trade deficit with China in advanced technology products was $190 billion. Testimony to Subcommittee on Trade by Patrick A. Mulloy in July 2006 asserted that we are slowly losing the advanced technology products industries to China.[3]
- *Security reviews:* The Chinese government can require security reviews of competitive technologies, which allows them to examine proprietary secrets and technologies.
- *Product testing:* This is another practice that is designed to access proprietary technology under the excuse of safety or standards.
- *Antimonopoly laws:* This is basically extortion, where the Chinese government can impose fines in order to force foreign companies to share their intellectual property (IP). An example is Qualcomm, an American company located in San Diego, California, which was fined $975 million because of monopoly complaints from Chinese smartphone manufacturers.
- *Dumping:* This occurs when China overproduces a product such as steel or solar panels and then dumps it into foreign markets at or below cost to gain market share.
- *Smuggling:* In 2013, U.S. Homeland Security detained nearly 3,000 people, some but not all of them from China, for trying to smuggle weapons and sensitive technologies out of the United States.
- *Ignoring patents:* Chinese leaders do not like America's patent laws and try to undermine them. So, some Chinese companies ignore patents and copy the technology knowing that the laws are difficult to enforce in China.
- *Acquisition of U.S. companies:* China also tries to acquire targeted technologies by acquiring U.S. companies or buying their stock.

---

[3] Testimony by P. Mulloy to the Subcommittee on Commerce on H.R. 5337 National Security Foreign Investment Reform. July 11, 2006. Washington, DC.

- *State-sponsored intellectual property theft:* IP theft includes cyber espionage, reverse engineering, counterfeiting, piracy, smuggling, and physical theft.
- *Evasion of export control laws:* These are laws designed to prevent the export of sensitive U.S. technologies with military applications. The espionage used to acquire these military technologies is a state-sponsored program which ignores the Arms Export Control Act.
- *Espionage:* According to the U.S. China Economic Panel Security Commission's 2015 report to Congress, "China's government conducts and sponsors a massive cyber espionage operation aimed at stealing trade secrets and intelligence from U.S. corporations and the government." The Chinese government funds ongoing programs to recruit operatives inside of U.S. companies to steal secrets. China has infiltrated, among many others, General Electric (wind turbine software), Monsanto (genetically modified corn), Avago (microchip technology), T-Mobile (core router software), Tennessee Valley Authority (nuclear material secrets), and Solar World (proprietary solar cell technology). A survey by the Center for International Studies lists 160 publicly reported instances of Chinese espionage directed at the United States since 2000.

This list illustrates what China views as acceptable business practices and what China will continue doing even if its leaders sign an agreement. In testimony before the Senate Small Business Committee, Bonnie Glaser, the Center for Strategic and International Studies' senior Asia adviser, said that "China steals more intellectual property than any other country." Chinese theft, she added, is "the single biggest threat to U.S. technology."

In a testimony to the Senate Intelligence committee, Bill Priestap, Assistant Director, Counterintelligence Division, Federal Bureau of Investigation, said,

Because the Chinese government creates an uneven playing field, and because this is done partly to facilitate the transfer of technology to China, our companies face what appears to be a very grim choice: participate and compete in the Chinese market and put vital corporate assets at grave risk, or neglect China and risk the loss of the second largest market in the world.

Priestap goes on to say,

While U.S. companies may be able to operate and profit in China for a time, it is on borrowed time. The Chinese government will permit foreign companies to operate only so long as it is advantageous to China. If a U.S. company is making a product that China needs but cannot yet produce domestically, such as sophisticated agricultural machinery? If so, the U.S. company will be allowed to operate, but only until China learns enough about the business that they can replace it with a domestic version.

Alternatively, a company may be allowed to operate simply to give China a better opportunity to understand how to copy the business and outcompete it globally. From the viewpoint of the Chinese government, many of the foreign companies doing business in China represent a temporary failure of the domestic market to meet demand. The government believes that if something can be made in China, then it should be made in China.[4]

We have become dependent on China: The COVID-19 crisis woke up the American populace to the danger of relying on China for medical products. I don't think the average citizen had any idea of just how many manufactured goods were transferred to China. It is now clear that the United States is dependent on China for a wide range of products, including medications, computers, electronics, cell phones, telecommunication equipment, household appliances, industrial machines, semiconductors, and generators to name just a few. Through an ongoing policy of

---

[4] B. Priestap, Assistant Director, Counter Intelligence Division, FBI. December 12, 2018. *China's Non-Traditional Espionage Against the United States.*

outsourcing plants and products to China, the United States has allowed China to steal its technologies and take over critical industries.

The COVID-19 pandemic has dramatically exposed the vulnerabilities of U.S. supply chains. U.S. government officials have been carrying out President Biden's executive order to propose remedies to the risks that such networks pose to four specific areas (pharmaceuticals, strategic materials such as rare earth minerals, semiconductors, and large-capacity batteries) and six sectors of the economy (defense, public health, communications technology, energy, transportation, and food production).

> *Pharmaceuticals:* After COVID-19 began, we found out that 90 percent of active pharmaceutical ingredients (API) come from either China or India. Quality oversight of China and India are poor which causes about two-thirds of the drug shortages. If China shuts the door on exports of medicines and their key ingredients, U.S. hospitals and clinics will cease to function within months. We are very vulnerable, and this is a security issue. There is no plan yet to make these ingredients domestically.
>
> The Biden administration announced that the Department of Health and Human Services will use the Defense Production Act to make a commitment of approximately $60 million to increase the production of API.
>
> *Medical products:* We also found out during the COVID-19 crisis that we could not ramp-up production of surgical masks, ventilators, and other needed medical equipment, because they had been sourced from China. The Trump administration asked textile manufacturers to invest in making masks and gowns in the United States and they did. But after 2020, The *New York Times* headline said "A Glut of Chinese Masks Is Driving U.S. Companies Out of Business." The government did not give the domestic producers long-term contracts, and hospitals found that they could buy them on the Internet (duty free) if the order was less than $800. So, manufacturers that were funded by the Trump administration at the beginning of the pandemic emergency are now going out of business or laying-off their workers. Most of the

personal protective equipment (PPE) products are again coming from China.

Mining minerals and metals are the front end of nearly every manufacturing supply chain, from smartphones and computer chips to renewable energy technologies and fighter jets. A recent article in *IndustryWeek* shows that China now controls 90 percent of the global supply of rare earth elements which are used everywhere in the digital economy: "We now find ourselves reliant on imports for nearly 50 essential minerals and metals and 100% reliant on imports for 18 of them."

Neodymium magnets: The United States is also dependent on these special magnet imports which are used in motors and many other devices for both defense and civilian uses. The Biden administration is looking into using Section 232 of the Trade Expansion Act of 1962 to make them domestically.

Auto parts: The U.S. auto industry has abandoned many of its domestic parts suppliers and is now the largest buyer of Chinese *auto parts* of the five countries who have large auto industries. An article by the Office of Industries revealed that in 2018, U.S. imports of automotive parts from China reached $15 billion for American assembly plants.[5] Since 2001 the U.S. has lost 1000 establishments and 211,803 employees in auto parts manufacturing. China is now the largest supplier of automotive parts in the world and exported $38.4 billion in 2018.

Semiconductors: China is stepping up efforts to become a major player in semiconductor design and manufacturing. If it succeeds, integrated-circuit companies around the world could face significant risks and opportunities. MNCs in every industry are clamoring to establish design centers in China to take advantage of China's growing need for microprocessors. Developing a world-class semiconductor industry is part of the "Made in China 2025" plan to serve both commercial and military agendas. An article in the National Interest says, "Yet, after years of being blocked from

---

[5] D. Coffin. August 2019. "China's Growing Role in U.S." *Automotive Supply Chains*, Office of Industries Working Paper ID-060.

acquiring the capability overseas, the Chinese government appears to be adapting, deploying a 'by all means necessary' strategy to achieve self-sufficiency in semiconductor R&D and production."[6] Semiconductor technologies should be declared national security technologies, and the MNCs should be prevented from giving them to the Chinese.

American manufacturers began offshoring production as early as the 1970s, which included information technology (IT), communications equipment, and a wide array of products from 38 manufacturing industries. According to an article in the Harvard Business Review, the primary goal of most MNCs was to "drive prices down, not ensure domestic supplies."[7] The public did not know how extensive this offshoring of critical product was until COVID-19 hit. The government is now faced with what to do about many critical products and supply chains that are now in China and are important to national security.

Negotiation won't work: I think negotiating with the Chinese communist government is an exercise in futility, and there is little chance China will change its methods and policies regardless of a signed agreement. In testifying recently to the Senate finance committee, U.S. trade Representative Robert Lighthizer said, "I don't know if tariffs alone will get them to stop cheating. I know one thing that won't work is talking to them." Dan Dimicco, former Chairman of the Coalition for a Prosperous America, said, "We have been down this road many times before, and Beijing has never actually changed course. The good news is that Trump's tariffs are taking a bite out of China's economy."

We have been through 21 years of China's excuses and promises about agreements, but I think the bottom line is that they can't stop cheating— it is endemic in their society. Unless we can make progress in stopping China's illegal and unfair trade practices, we cannot compete with them over the long haul and will lose the economic war. Accepting a status quo

---

[6] G. Levesque. June 18, 2018. "China Is Achieving Global Semiconductor Dominance," *The National Interest.*

[7] W. Shih, R. Huckman, and J. Wyner. May 26, 2021. "The Challenge of Rebuilding U.S. Domestic Supply Chains," *Harvard Business Review.*

with China today means they will eventually take our advanced technologies and dominate our major manufacturing industries.

If we continue to play the trade game based on China's rules, we will surely lose, endangering not just our economy but our whole society. China is the anaconda who is now totally wrapped around the U.S. body. Every breath we take allows them to tighten their grip, and eventually, we will be crushed and swallowed if we continue to play the trade game by China's rules.

China's 2025 plan: China has a 10-year plan called Made in China 2025, which "seeks to leverage the power of the Chinese state to promote indigenous innovation, advances technological self-sufficiency, and creates comparative advantage in key strategic sectors on a global scale." "Indigenous innovation" is a code phrase for innovation gained from others. Cities and counties receive subsidies and financial support from the government based on how much indigenous innovation they can bring into their geographic region, and it doesn't matter how they acquire the technology.

The 2025 plan includes the following goals:

1. Acquire key technologies and intellectual property from other countries.
2. Capture the emerging high-technology industries that will drive future economic growth. According to their 2025 plan, China wants to dominate advanced IT, automated machine tools, wind turbines, semiconductors, aircraft and aeronautical equipment, maritime vessels and marine engineering equipment, advanced rail equipment, electrical vehicles, electrical generation and transmission equipment, agricultural machinery and equipment, advanced materials, pharmaceuticals, and advance medical devices.

China has already swallowed the low-tech products we use to make. What they want now is our advanced technology products and all of the new technologies developed around them.

These technologies are found in America's 35 advanced technology industries (ATIs), including oil and gas, aerospace, biotechnology, life sciences, optoelectronics, communication weapons, computer systems, and software. The sector also includes nanotechnology, optics, additive manufacturing, advanced materials, advanced robotics, big data analytics, cloud computing, the Internet of Things, autonomous vehicles, and genomics. If we lose the technologies in these industries through IP theft or multinational companies outsourcing, we will lose our economic future. So, the big question is how can we stop them?

Penalties: In January 2022, the news media was awash with stories about the shortages of consumer goods, including the critical medical goods and pharmaceuticals mentioned earlier. These shortages will hopefully serve as a wake-up call for where America is in terms of dependence on imports. There are stories about the U.S. ports not being able to unload ships, not enough trucks or drivers, spiraling shipping costs, and the dependence on rogue countries like China.

The solution is not to find other foreign exporters, but it is to reclaim these manufacturing sectors and to become more self-sufficient. The good news is that many American manufacturers are demonstrating the advantages of domestic suppliers and many are beginning to reshore. Doing so, could help reduce the dangerous dependence on China.

The first step is to recognize China as *a competitor not a trading partner*, and do everything possible to stop this competitor from gaining strategic and tactical advantages. We need a plan like China's "Made in China 2025" plan that describes all of the technologies and manufacturing industries that we must protect if we are really going to compete using a strategy of innovation.

And, of course, there is always the simple solution of reciprocity. Why don't we just ask China to reciprocate? Clyde Prestowitz suggests in his book *The World Turned Upside Down* that "The openness of U.S. society combined with the tightly closed nature of China enables Beijing to exploit American openness in ways that undermine free world values generally, and American economic, technological, and military values specifically." Why should China be able to charge a 19 percent value-added tax (VAT) when the United States has no VAT? Why should China be able to buy our currency and keep our dollar high when they don't allow procurement of their currency? The answer is that China wants to play the game using their own rules and always having the advantage. So why not begin a strategy of reciprocity?

The United States is beginning to fight back and compile lists of Chinese companies that won't play by the rules. These lists should include any Chinese company found guilty of using any of the 16 cheating methods explained previously. Also, companies which are a threat to our national security and companies with ties to the People's Liberation Army, surveillance technologies, or involved in human rights abuses. We can't stop China's mercantilist strategies, but we can stop companies who are on the list from exporting to America and access to our markets.

We can't stop the Chinese from forcing American companies into forced technology transfer agreements, but we can put our advanced technologies on a national security list that can't be manufactured outside of the United States. We can also stop China from accessing American university research labs or contracting with American scientists on work that affects our national security. The government could also offer tax incentives for American corporations to reshore their production or find better foreign vendors. We could also assess fines on all State Owned Enterprises (SOEs) that are subsidized by the Chinese government to enable them to dump products into America below cost or to simply deny their products from going through customs.

The mood in Congress is changing, and there are now many bills that could stop or reduce China cheating such as:

- House Ways and Means Chairman, Earl Blumenauer, introduced a bill titled the *Import Security and Fairness Act* which would reduce the value of merchandise considered "de minimis" and get through customs duty free. The value of goods sold on the Internet that are duty free is now $800 but would be reduced to $200 if this act is passed.
- A bill titled *Chips for America* was passed by the Senate and included $52 billion in federal investments for domestic semiconductor research, design, and manufacturing. The bill has passed the Senate and includes a 25 percent tax credit to build fabs in the U.S. However an anti China security measure was removed from the bill which would have barred companies from manufacturing chips in China.

- The Country of Origin Labeling Online Act (COOL) would require Amazon and other e-commerce sites to display the origin of the goods. This bill is still being debated by Congress and is being strongly resisted by the retail lobby. The COOL bill never got out of committee to be voted on by the Senate.
- *The Holding Foreign Companies Accountable Act* was passed in 2021 and now must be implemented at the SEC. The new law protects U.S. investors by prohibiting Chinese and other foreign companies from being listed on U.S. security exchanges if the company has failed to comply with a (Public Company Accounting and Oversight Board) audit. However, the law does not cover 4,200 A-share companies that are now in passive investment products in the portfolios of U.S. investors.
- The Made in America Office of the Office of Management and Budget (OMB) has unveiled a new *Buy America* transparency process affecting 24 federal agencies and $600 billion annual procurement. The Buy America program was implemented under President Biden's Executive Order 14005.
- The U.S. steel and aluminum industries were saved from China dumping by the *Section 232 tariffs*, but China and EU lobbyists are pressuring the government to eliminate the tariffs.
- For most Chinese goods the only defense the United States has for protection are the *Trump 301 tariffs under Trade Act of 1974*. But there are 549 different products that have negotiated exclusions, and the pressure is on the Biden administration to accept more exclusions. Until some of these other bills can be passed by Congress, the only protection we have are the 301 tariffs and they should be extended.
- President Biden's *Executive order 14032* expanded capital market sanctions on Chinese companies to include defense-related companies and Chinese companies that develop surveillance technology to facilitate repression of serious human rights abuses.

- The new Uyghur Forced Labor law banning all imports from Xinxiang Province that are closely identified as coming from forced labor was passed by Congress January 6, 2022. The new law will add 14 Chinese companies to the entity list and five others for aiding the China Armed Forces.
- The U.S. Court of International Trade (CIT) removed the Section 201 tariffs on bifacial solar panels that put in jeopardy U.S. solar panel makers. However, the Coalition for a Prosperous America has urged the Biden administration to file an appeal, but the request has fallen on deaf ears.
- The Congress needs to sanction individual companies that cheat, like the recent sanctioning of Huawei. On May 17, 2020, the U.S. sanctioned Huawei and its 67 affiliates in 26 countries to limit their access to U.S. suppliers. The Justice Department is also prosecuting Huawei for bank fraud, technology theft, and violating the U.S. Sanctions against Iran.

China's reaction to all of these bills is to use climate change as a battering ram to reverse attempts to hold them accountable. According to the Coalition for a Prosperous America, China is saying, "No climate negotiations, no phase two trade negotiations, until sanctions, including capital market sanctions and the Commerce Department's Entity List Restrictions on some Chinese companies like Huawei, are removed." Chen Weihua, the China Daily EU Bureau, made the China trade position crystal clear. He said,

> Unilateral U.S. trade actions, especially in the name of national security, have not only violated global rules but created obstacles for resolving critical bilateral trade issues. It is time for the Biden administration to revoke those policies, starting with lifting Trump's punitive tariffs and stopping the trade war against China.

Instead of attempting to negotiate some kind of compromise to reduce their cheating, the Chinese Communist Party CCP's reaction is always to retaliate or threaten the other party. We are at another crossroads with

China. The Biden administration has passed several laws to stop China from cheating. So the question is now whether the administration is going to enforce the laws or fall back into a policy of forbearance.

The Wall Street/China problem: Wall Street's never-ending pursuit of profits at any cost has resulted in their continuous investment in Chinese companies even if they are on the U.S. government's entity list. When it comes to profit seeking, they apparently just cannot help themselves.

We are in an economic struggle with China, and they are using all of the tools available to their authoritarian regime to overtake us. However, many of the large financial firms on Wall Street are pursuing their own short-term interests rather than what is good for the nation's future. They don't seem to acknowledge (or don't care) that investing in Chinese companies is really investing in a police state.

Financial firms such as Vanguard, Blackrock, and others continue to invest in Chinese companies that are on the Department of Commerce's entity list as well as companies who are part of the China Military Industrial Complex. Blackrock is the world's largest asset manager and surprisingly recommended in 2021 that investors triple their allocations in Chinese assets.[8]

For example, it is now well known that China has engaged in facial recognition, voice recognition, forced sterilization, forced labor, and reeducation camps to control the Uyghur population in Xinjiang Province. The American Investment firm T. Rowe Price was an investor in Hikvision (a surveillance technology company), and Hoshine Silicon was part of three of Vanguard's mutual funds' portfolios. Five polysilicon Chinese companies that make material for their solar panel industries are in Xinjiang Province and have been added to the Commerce Department's entity list, but two of them, Hoshine Silicon Industry and Xinjiang Daqo Energy, are traded on U.S. exchanges via passive investment products. The vast majority of American investors are unaware that their mutual funds include Chinese companies that are not compliant to U.S. laws. American Financial firms Blackrock, Invesco, Goldman Sachs, Vanguard,

---

[8] N. Iacovella. January 5, 2020. "CPA to SEC Chairman Gensler: Prohibit Index Providers from Including U.S. Sanctioned Chinese Companies," *Coalition for a Prosperous America.*

and State Street own over 18 million shares of Chinese companies on the entity list. Blackrock alone owns $600 million in Daqo.

The Biden administration is trying to prevent American investors from buying stock in companies tied to China's military industrial complex. Eight of these Chinese companies were recently added to the entity list that were assisting Chinese military's quantum computing efforts, which support military applications such as counter-stealth and counter submarine applications, and the ability to break encryption codes.[9]

The Biden administration also recently added the Chinese company Sense Time to the entity list because it is connected to the CCP's human rights abuses and supports the Chinese People's Liberation Army. The list also includes Huawei, which is a huge telecom manufacturer, China National Offshore Oil, and Semiconductor Manufacturing International, who wants to dominate the world semiconductor market. The American public is only now waking up to the fact that the Communist party's efforts to surveil their citizens and conduct human rights abuses is on an Orwellian scale and is a real threat to our national security.

The U.S. government is progressing in adding Chinese companies to the Commerce Department entity list, but the progress is slow. So far, Wall Street only cooperates when a company is added to the entity list. According to the Coalition for a Prosperous America, there are 4,200 unregulated Chinese companies in the investment portfolios of scores of unwitting retail investors, and in a letter to Janet Yellen, they said, "What are you going to do about this outrageous level of largely unregulated American Investor funding of a totalitarian police state."[10] Even though Biden's executive order said that it was to "ensure that U.S. investments are not supporting Chinese companies that undermine the security of values of the United States and our allies," Wall Street continues to put profit before country.

China is using all of its tools as an authoritarian government to try and overtake us. I think that our only competitive hope is to devise our

---

[9] K. Rapoza. December 6, 2021. "Why Is Wall Street Still Investing in Blacklisted China Companies?" *Coalition for a Prosperous America.*

[10] Z. Mottl. Chairman. January 10, 2022. "CPA Letter to Secretary Yellen Regarding Protecting American Investors from Risky, Dangerous A-Share Investments in Chinese Companies," *Coalition for a Prosperous America.*

own long-term strategy to combat China's unfair trade practices and protect the technologies invented in America. But, this would require the support of MNCs.

Decoupling from China: If China remains intransigent and is not willing or able to change its mercantilist methods, then the only practical alternative is to begin the process of decoupling from China. This process has already begun with Trump's tariffs, and there is support for decoupling from Republican Senators like Josh Hawley, Tom Cotton, and Marco Rubio and Democratic Senators Tammy Baldwin and Mark Warner and others.

China's "Made in China 2025" plan, according to U.S. Senator Josh Hawley, is a plan that "seeks to remake the world in its own image and to bend the global economy to its will." The China plan describes which industries they want to dominate and which technologies they are after to achieve their goals. The problem is that instead of investing in designing and manufacturing their own technologies, they have developed methods to acquire these technologies through forced technology transfer agreements, IP theft, and industrial espionage.

After decades of our government and U.S. MNCs advocating the outsourcing of American products and jobs—and touting the advantages of importing cheap Chinese products—it is time to face up to the fact that these policies have led to deindustrialization, lower wages, a shrinking manufacturing sector, and a threat to our national security.

The problems of the WTO: The WTO was created in 1995 to replace the post-WWII General Agreement on Tariffs. Many American corporations have benefitted from the governance of the WTO, but it has been very lax in regulating countries who break the rules, like China. In fact, the WTO has become a joke in terms of pretending to administer trade, while China freely violates trade rules claiming to be in accord with the law.

In 2020, Senator Josh Hawley, R-Mo., published a dramatic proposal to abolish the WTO. He introduced a joint resolution in the Senate that would begin America's withdrawal from that organization. Hawley said, "The global economic system as we know it is a relic; it requires reform, top to bottom. We should begin with one of its leading institutions, the World Trade Organization. We should abolish it."

Another solution is for the industrialized liberal democracies being undermined by Red China to simply withdraw, start their own organization, and leave the WTO to irrelevance. The WTO as currently organized works well for American multinationals who import or who have plants in China, but it does very little to stop China's mercantilist policies or protect American advanced technologies and workers.

Multinationals will oppose any solution on China: For decades, American MNCs have been willing to sell out to the CCP, to enhance their own strategies for short-term profits and shareholder value. They have been willing to sacrifice American manufacturing, jobs, suppliers, industries, and communities in this Faustian bargain. I think it goes without saying that most American MNCs will oppose decoupling, but they are going to be pressured to change because the politics regarding China are changing in the U.S. Congress. I think the MNCs might cooperate if the government can give them some relief from forced technology transfer and some protection of their products and markets. Big-box retailers like Walmart and Target source many of their products from China and will not want to upset their supply chains. But if the tariffs on the consumer products become permanent, or are expanded to more products, they may think twice.

America is at a crossroads. We must stop dealing with China as we hope they would be and begin dealing with them as they are. The United States is in a favorable position in the struggle because China needs our consumer markets more than we need theirs. It is not an exaggeration to say we are in the beginning of a cold war with China and must defend ourselves just as we did with the Soviet Union. Accepting the status quo like we did for 21 years is no longer an option. Decoupling will be a long, slow, and contentious process; but it is time to face reality and do something for the country, our citizens, and American manufacturing. We need short-term sacrifice to avoid long-term collapse.

Now, I know the free-market capitalists will scream protectionism and criticize any effort to penalize or tax Chinese imports. But they do not offer any solutions to the growing list of Chinese problems listed in this chapter. I think this problem is at least as threatening as the war on terror because China now has the power to kill our economy. It is time to stand up to China.

CHAPTER 15

Decline of Productivity and GDP Growth

There is a strong sense in America today that something is seriously wrong in our economy, particularly for citizens with only a high school diploma. It is based on fear and anger and has resulted in populism, nationalism, and conspiracy theories being on the rise. Most people don't realize that their economic struggles are connected to the reduction in productivity and GDP growth, and the 40-year acceptance of increasing trade deficits and the commitment to cheap imports.

Labor productivity, defined as output per labor hour, has grown at below the average rate since 2005. Figure 15.1 shows productivity growth since 1994. But since 2005, the average annual productivity growth rate is 1.3 percent—well under the average of 2.1 percent going back to 1947. The government is not sure why the productivity growth is so weak, but a decrease in capital investment, income inequality, and reduction in innovation caused by increased foreign competition from China are primary factors. The primary reason that productivity growth is important is that weak productivity growth results in slow economic growth and a decline in wages, profits, and living standards.

The U.S. Bureau of Labor Statistics says that this slowdown has resulted in the cumulative loss of $10.9 trillion in output in the nonfarm business sector. This corresponds to a loss of $95,000 in output per worker. In the fourth quarter of 2021, productivity fell at an annual rate of 4.2 percent, the largest quarterly reduction in 40 years. What is going on?

An example of how productivity growth affects wages is a study by the Economics Policy Institute. The study shows that during the period between 1979 and 2019, productivity grew 59.7 percent, while workers compensation grew by only 15.9 percent. As shown in Chapter 3 on the

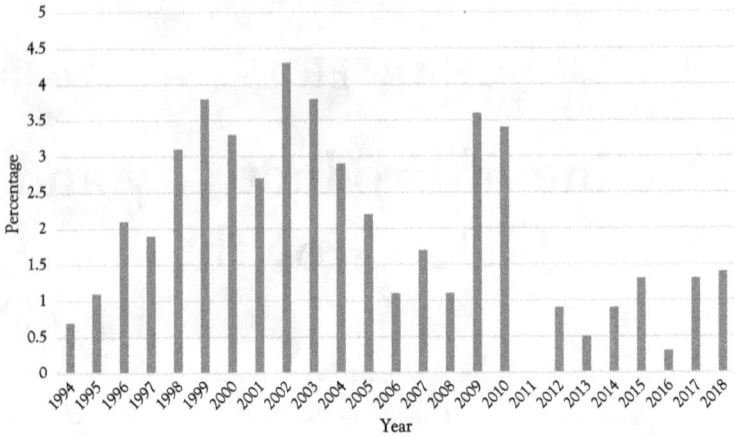

Figure 15.1 Labor productivity growth, 1994 to 2018

Source: Bureau of Labor Statistics, Labor Productivity Growth: annual percent changes, nonfarm business sector, 1994 to 2018.

growth of inequality, the top 10 percent, and especially the top 1 percent of all earners, gained the lion share of all compensation during the last 40 years.[1] Chapter 3 also shows that the compensation of the middle class declined from a high of 53.21 percent in 1970 to 45.8 percent in 2020.

The primary cause of reduced productivity and economic growth is globalization and deindustrialization. When policy makers and industry leaders decided to go all out for aggregate growth and free trade agreements (FTAs) without any industry protection, it put American manufacturing up against workers in low-cost countries. This meant workers were competing with hourly wages of $3 per hour in Mexico and $1 per hour in Vietnam with no protection. So began 40 years of outsourcing in an economic game we could not win. It also meant we would open the floodgates of imported products and endorse a policy of financing the trade deficit ad infinitum. In essence, we gave up on exports, and there has been little to no government program or even a goal to reduce the trade deficit or to restrict the flood of imports.

---

[1] L. Mishel. September 2, 2021. "Growing Inequalities, Reflecting Growing Employer Power, Have Generated a Productivity Pay Gap Since 1979," *Working Economics Blog*, Economic Policy Institute.

Gross Domestic Product Growth

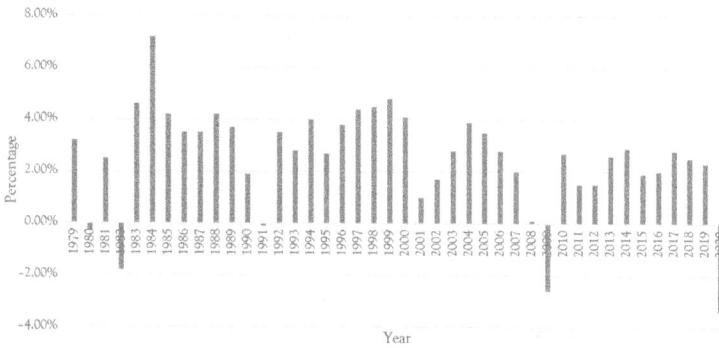

Figure 15.2 *GDP annual growth, 1979 to 2019*

Source: World Bank, www.macrotrends.net/countries/USA/united-states/gdp-growth-rate

Figure 15.2 shows gross domestic product (GDP) growth percentages back to 1979. There were several decades where the United States enjoyed 3 to 4 percent GDP growth, but since 2000, it has been an anemic 1.8 percent.

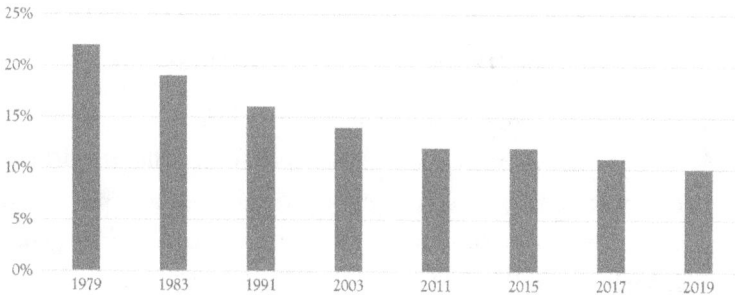

Figure 15.3 *Manufacturing share of GDP, 1979 to 2019*

Source: Department of Labor Statistics, Federal Reserve Bank of St. Louis, April 2017.

Figure 15.3 is the manufacturing sector's share of GDP growth and is similar to the chart on the decline of productivity in that the manufacturing share has also been declining for 40 years. Manufacturing was 22 percent of GDP in 1979 but declined to 10 percent by 2019.

A trade deficit occurs when a country imports more goods and services than it exports. The macroeconomic explanations and justifications for trade deficits are often convoluted and do not make sense to the average voter.

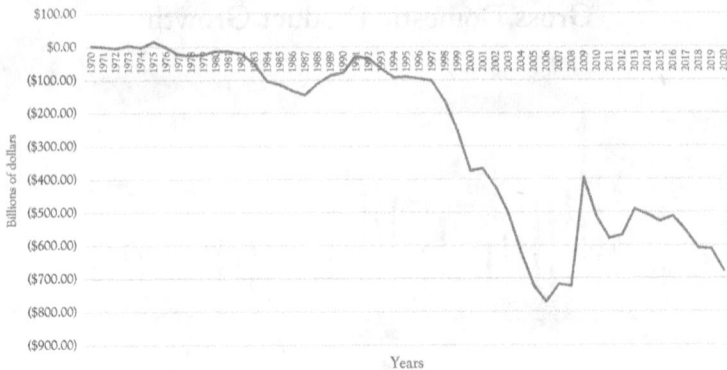

Figure 15.4 U.S. trade balance, 1970 to 2019

Source: U.S. Census Bureau, Economic Indicator Division, U.S. Trade in Goods and Services—Balance of Payments, value in millions of dollars 1970 to 2020.

Figure 15.4 shows that the United States has been running trade deficits for 40 years and that they went above $400 billion after China was allowed into the WTO in 2001.

All of these figures seem to indicate that in 1979 America reached the "high noon" of the American Century and we have been declining ever since.

Pro-Trade Deficit Arguments

There are many economists who support trade deficits because they believe that the overall aggregate benefit is worth financing the deficits. They know that we might lose jobs and even industries, but they believe the aggregate benefits to the economy are worth the losses, and they prefer to ignore trade deficits.

Michael Froman, a former trade representative, is a good example of the aggregate argument. He says, "every legitimate economist says that measuring trade policy by the size of the goods deficit is probably not a passing grade in basic economics class." Mr. Froman was a chief negotiator for the Trans-Pacific trade agreement, which was killed by former President Donald Trump. Trump's decision to kill the TPP was right because it would have been a repeat of NAFTA and all of the manufacturing losses.

Another example is an article in *Forbes* Magazine titled "41 Straight Years of Trade Deficits Yet America Still Stands Strong." The author, Dan Ikenson, says, "Rather than a reflection of weakness or stupidity or profligacy or foreign malfeasance, the annual trade deficit is a sign of U.S. economic hegemony—a global endorsement of the relative strength of the U.S. economy and its direction." He goes on to say that "During those 41 straight years of trade deficits, the size of the U.S. economy tripled in real terms, real manufacturing value added quadrupled, and the number of jobs in the economy almost doubled, outpacing growth in the civilian workforce."

His argument, like many economists, is based on Americans consuming cheap imported products, which saves them money to spend elsewhere in the economy. This view also makes the case that deficits are good because they can be financed by borrowing from the very countries that are exporting to the United States or as Ikenson says,

> But here's the most important part. In all cases, the dollars that go abroad to purchase foreign goods and services (imports) and foreign assets (outward investment) are matched almost perfectly by dollars coming back to the United States to purchase U.S. goods and services (exports) and U.S. assets (inward investment).

Perhaps, the best argument in support of trade deficits comes from the Hoover Institute. Russ Roberts of the Institute summarizes his aggregate argument by saying,

> By directing resources to where the economy is most competitive, it creates new opportunities and society-wide advances that improve life for everyone in unforeseen ways. Rather than protecting struggling industries, he says, policy should focus on giving people the skills to compete and flourish.

The Downside of Trade Deficits

The struggling industries are manufacturing industries and the losers are manufacturing employees, their families, and communities. Roberts also makes it sound easy to give the losers of trade deficits the skills to compete or find another job. But after 30 years of debate and six major skilled worker studies, we still have not developed the training programs to help the millions of people who have lost their jobs because of trade deficits and outsourcing, or even to train the skilled workers needed to replace the retirees.

The economists that support free trade and trade deficits so that we can import cheap goods seldom mention the downside of trade deficits or admit that millions of people have lost their jobs, the hollowing out of the manufacturing industry, or the costs of carrying $12 trillion of financed debt. And they never mention the role that America's MNCs have played by aggressively outsourcing production and jobs to low-cost foreign countries. They use plants in other countries to not only serve foreign markets but also ship their products back to the U.S. market. For example, most of the car manufacturers now have plants in Mexico, and Mexico now exports more cars to the United States than the United States exports to the rest of the world.

The trading system has become unbalanced and is biased in favor of investor rights and binding dispute mechanisms, whereas workers, consumers, and environmentalists have been left out.

The Twin Secrets of Economic Growth

In his report "The Twin Secrets of Economic Growth" economist Jeff Ferry of the Coalition for a Prosperous America says that "the evidence suggests that two important indicators provide the best explanation of the secrets of economic growth. Those indicators are the share of a nation's GDP devoted to manufacturing, and the level of the current account balance as a share of GDP." Importantly, Ferry provides data that makes it clear that "manufacturing is a key contributor to growth because it is the only sector that can create multi-decade broad-based increases in labor productivity, which is the key to rising wages." Ferry goes on to say that "the opposite is true because a nation with a significant current account deficit is always in trouble because it is losing share of either its foreign market or its domestic market or both."[2]

---

[2] J. Ferry. September 21, 2021. "The Twin Secrets of Economic Growth," *The Coalition for a Prosperous America.*

The United States has had 41 years of trade deficits accumulating $12 trillion in debt financing the deficits. We are in a serious jam because America's political leaders and MNCs have favored increasing trade and financing deficits, despite the loss of jobs, suppliers, and industries. Most of the gains have gone to the top 10 percent of all earners and resulted in serious inequality as well as a decline of American manufacturing. It also results in loss of economic growth as shown in Figure 15.2.

The justification for continuing to finance trade deficits has been that importing low-cost foreign products for consumers will save them money that they can spend elsewhere in the economy. It also serves retailers and manufacturers that depend on imports. But to achieve this, America had to sacrifice manufacturing industries and manufacturing jobs, finance $12 trillion in deficits, and become the biggest debtor nation and the biggest importer in the world. Consequently, America now suffers from low productivity and a decline in GDP growth.

The only answer as pointed out in Jeff Ferry's article is to refocus on increasing manufacturing's share of GDP and to reduce the trade deficit.

One of the best summaries of these problems was described by former U.S. Ambassador Robert Lighthizer, who, as the U.S. Trade Representative, was out on the economic front lines of our trade problems for many years. Lighthizer wrote an op-ed piece for *The Economist* Magazine where he advocated keeping the tariffs as a trade tool and describing the dangers of ever-increasing trade deficits and the danger of a strong dollar. He railed against America's trade agreements and said that the benefits had all gone to global corporations, at the expense of blue-collar workers and small and midsize companies.

He begins his article by stating that the United States has accumulated more than $12 trillion in global deficits since 2001. There doesn't seem to be any plan or even discussion by the government on trying to change this economic problem to achieving a surplus instead of a deficit. But anyone who has taken economics 101 knows that countries are supposed to eventually get back to a surplus because the dollar value is supposed to go down making our exports more competitive. But this hasn't happened for a variety of reasons. Here is a brief summary of some of Lighthizer's primary points.

- The United States is now the largest importer in the world which has caused us to also be the world's largest debtor nation.
- Our ongoing trade deficits have shipped $trillions of wealth to foreign countries in return for foreign goods, and our foreign competitors use the money to purchase our assets and debt instruments. Lighthizer said "in a real sense America is trading ownership of its productive assets and economic future for short term consumption."[3]
- The purchase of securities like stocks, corporate bonds, and Treasury bonds makes for greater demand for dollar assets thus driving up the strength of the dollar.
- Wall Street loves a strong dollar because it means more sales of stocks and bonds, but the strong dollar is at the heart of the trade deficit problem.
- Lighthizer's solution is for the government to tax capital inflows using a Market Access Charge to disincentivize foreigners from buying American assets and lower the value of the dollar.
- He also suggests raising tariffs selectively. He suggests imposing tariffs on all imports and then selectively raising or lowering the tariffs depending on whether deficit for the product is going up or down. As the trade deficit is slowly reduced, the tariffs for the product would be reduced or eliminated.

There is a strong sense in America today that something is seriously wrong in our economy, particularly citizens with only a high school diploma or less. It is based on fear and anger and has resulted in populism, nationalism, and conspiracy theories being on the rise. Most people don't realize that their economic struggles are connected to the reduction in productivity and GDP growth, the 40-year acceptance of increasing trade deficits, and the commitment to cheap imports. Unless the government and industry leaders decide to do something about it, I am afraid

---

[3] R. Lighthizer. October 5, 2021. *Robert Lighthizer on the Need for Tariffs to Reduce America's Trade Deficit, The Economist* Magazine.

the country is in for a hard economic landing. Robert Lighthizer sums it up with his comment from *The Economist* article. He says, "International trade has largely failed America over the past three decades. Indeed, it is slowly bleeding the country to death."

U.S. MNCs have hacked a prime cut out of the carcass of America, and it is about time they pitch in and help us out of the mess they and the government have created.

CHAPTER 16

The Truth About Currency Manipulation and a Strong Dollar

Economists know that our foreign competitors manipulate their currencies to keep the dollar overvalued which fuels our trade deficit. Strong lobbying groups, ranging from retail importers to Wall Street, spend huge amounts of lobbying money to pressure Congress to maintain the status quo and do nothing about these problems. The big losers are the manufacturing and agriculture sectors. Unless the government and industry leaders decide to do something about it, I am afraid the country is in for some bad, future economic problems.

Currency manipulation is back in the news. After the Trump administration designated Switzerland, Taiwan, and Vietnam as currency manipulators in 2020, the Biden administration has reversed the decisions, even as Switzerland, Taiwan, and Vietnam met thresholds for the label.

The Treasury Department said that those "three economies *met criteria* for the manipulator label, including a large trade surplus with the U.S." But it said that there was "insufficient evidence" to conclude that the three trading partners showed the intent of "preventing effective balance of payments adjustments or gaining unfair competitive advantage in international trade to apply the tag."

The new assessments signal that the Biden administration is taking a less confrontational approach to international currency policy and probably also signals that they are going to be unwilling to do anything about the overvalued dollar. In fact, Treasury Secretary Janet Yellen said, "the value of the dollar should be determined by markets, and the targeting of exchange rates for commercial advantage by other countries was 'unacceptable'."

This is a contradiction to President Biden's promises in his Build Back Better program because trade deficits, currency manipulation, and the strong dollar are economic forces that directly affect the future of American manufacturing and agriculture. Let's look at why we must face the truth and do something about these issues, regardless of the politics.

Currency Manipulation

The leading cause of U.S. trade deficits is currency manipulation and misalignment by China and 15 other trading countries. Currency manipulation happens when one of our trading partners buys up U.S. assets such as U.S. Treasury notes and bonds, which make the value of the dollar artificially high. By making the dollar more expensive, it makes our exports more expensive and makes the foreign countries' products cheaper. Currency manipulation is illegal under the rules of the International Monetary Fund and the WTO, but the rules are never enforced.

According to economic theory, running deficits over many years is supposed to weaken our currency and eventually reduce the dollar value and reduce our deficit. The thinking goes like this: A trade deficit creates downward pressure on a country's currency under a floating exchange rate regime. With a cheaper domestic currency, imports become more expensive in the country with the trade deficit. But it isn't happening in America. We have been running trade deficits for more than 40 years, and they get worse every year. The trade deficits get worse because our competitors manipulate currencies to keep the dollar value high.

I know that there are guidelines that the Treasury Department uses to define who is a currency manipulator and they go out of their way to not put our trading partners on the list. But if you look at the list of the top 15 countries shown in Table 16.1, the obvious question is why do we run deficits and they all have surpluses and buy American assets so we can finance these deficits. Isn't this currency manipulation when they do it because they know it will give their exports a price advantage and

Table 16.1 Trade deficits with 15 trading partners

Year to date trade deficits with 15 trading partners as of October 2020			
Rank	Country	U.S. deficit ($billions)	Country surplus, April 2021 ($billions)
1.	China	−253	+311
2.	Mexico	−92.2	+113
3.	Vietnam	−56.6	+70
4.	Switzerland	−51.1	+57
5.	Germany	−46.2	+57
6.	Ireland	−46.1	+56
7.	Japan	−42.8	+55
8.	Malaysia	−25.3	+32
9.	Taiwan	−24.1	+30
10.	Italy	−22.6	+30
11.	Thailand	−21.7	+26
12.	India	−19.5	+24
13.	South Korea	−19.3	+25
14.	France	−12.1	+12
15.	Canada	−11.6	+2.5

Source: U.S. Census Department—Foreign Trade Data.

they know that the United States will do nothing about it. These surplus countries in effect loan us money to pay for our excess of imports over exports, which in effect transfers employment from the United States to other countries.

The government has known about currency manipulation for decades but no politician—Democrat or Republican—has been willing to face the truth and do something about it.

In 2008, President Barack Obama, in a campaign appearance, said that if China continued its currency manipulation, the United States would cut off market access. And when Donald Trump was running for office in 2016, he promised that he would "declare China a currency manipulator" on the first day of his presidency. But when they got into office, nothing happened.

Currency manipulation is by far the most protectionist international economic policy in the 21st century, but, even though it is illegal, neither the U.S. government, the International Monetary Fund, nor the World Trade Organization (WTO) has been willing to really do anything about it.

According to the Economic Policy Institute, "Currency misalignment is the single largest cause of growing U.S. trade deficits. U.S. trade can be rebalanced, creating millions of good manufacturing jobs, by lowering the value of the dollar by about 25 percent." The failure to end currency misalignment was a major cause of *GM's decision* to close five manufacturing plants and outsource production, eliminating 12,000 jobs, and *Ford's plan* to reduce its workforce by 12 percent, eliminating 24,000 jobs.

In April 2021, the Biden administration redesignated Vietnam and Switzerland; they were removed from the currency manipulator list and moved to enhanced monitoring list. It appears that no politician, particularly no President, is going to do anything about currency manipulation. I think they fear that it would raise the prices of cheap imported goods, which could lose them votes and jeopardize their reelection.

America's MNCs also want the status quo. They use their lobbying power and political influence to forestall any attempts to legislate any solutions to currency manipulation and the overvalued dollar. The big importers and companies with plants in Asia benefit from cheap Asian labor and artificial foreign prices and have no interest in changing the current system.

To their credit, the Trump administration tried to stop China from currency manipulation by imposing unilateral trade sanctions under Section 301 of the 1974 trade act. In 2019, they increased the 2018 tariffs on $200 billion in Chinese goods from 10 to 25 percent. But these tariffs only affect China so far, it has not motivated China to come to the negotiating table to discuss currency manipulation or any of their mercantilist cheating tools.

To be fair, I must admit that government has not always ignored the currency manipulation problem. In 1971, Richard Nixon assessed a 10 percent surcharge that coerced our trading partners to raise the value of their currencies. In the 1985 Plaza Accords, President Reagan forced both Japan and Germany to stop manipulation, which resulted in a 30 percent drop in the value of the dollar. Nixon and Reagan proved that the government can successfully intervene on these problems, but since the 1980s, no administration has done anything about currency manipulation or the overvalued dollar.

One of the reasons that foreign countries are so willing to finance our deficit is that American tax law subsidizes it. The *Coalition for a Prosperous America* (CPA) says that other countries invest in America because they don't have to pay any taxes on the earnings, and as a bonus, "the American government often avoids reporting the income to their home country tax collector."

Strong Dollar

The trade deficit is symptomatic of an even greater issue—the dollar's strength and reserve status. The high value of the dollar since the 1990s has acted like a massive tax on U.S. exports and a huge subsidy to U.S. imports.[1] In the last 10 years, the dollar has risen in value 25.5 percent.[2] Many of the currency manipulator country's economies have large economic surpluses which allows them to purchase U.S. securities like corporate bonds, stocks, and U.S. government debt. According to the CPA, in the first 10 months of 2021, capital purchases of U.S. securities were $409 billion. This allows our competitors to both keep the dollar strong, weakening our manufacturing and agriculture sectors, and use the United States as a tax shelter.

According to the London-based nonprofit, the Tax Justice Network, the U.S. ranks second only to the Cayman islands as a tax shelter for foreign investors who want to avoid paying taxes in their own country.[3] According to the U.S Treasury, the U.S. debt to foreigners totaled $21 trillion as of June 2021, and with a goods trade deficit that went over

---

[1] R. Blecker. June 1, 2003. *The Benefits of a Lower Dollar*, Economic Policy Institute.

[2] Based on the Federal Reserve board's Nominal U.S. Dollar Index (DTWEXBGS).

[3] Tax Justice Network, Financial Secrecy Index. 2020. *Narrative Report on United States of America*, p. 5.

$1 trillion in 2021, nobody seems to worry about how we could pay back this debt.[4]

Politicians and government administrations are especially afraid to address government policy on the value of the dollar. In 1994, the new treasury secretary of the Clinton administration, Robert Rubin, said, "A strong dollar is in our national interest," because it would assure foreign investors that Washington would not interfere in exchange markets to debase the currency. Rubin, like most treasury secretaries in recent times, was from Wall Street, and Wall Street has more to gain from a strong dollar than any other business or political group.

Since Rubin, every treasury secretary has supported the strong dollar policy. In 2006, Hank Paulson, treasury secretary for George W. Bush, said the benefits of a strong dollar are lower interest rates, more liquid financial markets, cheaper funding for American banks, and the ability to run large trade deficits. In 2010, Treasury Secretary Tim Geithner tabled a report showing that stopping China's currency manipulation would help create one million U.S. jobs. In the Trump administration, Treasury Secretary Steven Mnuchin admitted that a weak dollar would be good for exports but he didn't label China a currency manipulator until late in 2019. And in 2021, Treasury Secretary Janet Yellen has fallen in line with all previous Treasury officials and does not want to do anything about the strong dollar or currency manipulation. It appears that anyone coming from the financial sector will always have the same view, which results in an anti-manufacturing policy, and deindustrialization.

Everybody knows that the dollar is overvalued, but there is enormous pressure from many business interests to keep it high. Strong lobbying groups, ranging from retail importers to Wall Street, will spend huge amounts of lobbying money to pressure Congress to maintain the status quo and do nothing about these problems.

A study in 2015 by the Peterson Institute argued that the problems of currency manipulation and currency misalignment are acute. The author says that every 10 percent rise in the dollar value adds $350 billion to the

---

[4] J. Ferry, CPA. January 3, 2022. *Trillion-Dollar Capital Flows Into the U.S. Are Driven By Tax avoidance, Trading, and a Tiny Bit of Real Investment.*

trade deficit and reduces overall economic growth by 1.65 percent with a corresponding job loss of 1.5 million jobs.[5]

A new working paper from the CPA called "Imports Growth and Job Creation from a Competitive Dollar" reveals what could positively result if the dollar value could be reduced. The econometric model is over a six-year period and shows that the dollar price adjustment necessary to achieve a current account balance is a reduction of 27 percent. If the dollar value could be reduced this much, it would result in:

1. Gross Domestic Product growth of 1.2 percentage points per year higher than baseline growth which is an additional $1 trillion.
2. 5.2 million additional jobs by 2024 and 1.5 million would be in manufacturing.
3. Export growth five times faster than baseline, while imports would grow more slowly.[6]

President Biden's administration promised to "mobilize American manufacturing and innovation to ensure that the future is made in America," according to Biden's website. In recent speeches, Biden also says he "plans to build a strong industrial base and small-business-led supply chains to retain and create millions of good-paying union jobs in manufacturing and technology." These statements, however, are a direct contradiction to his financial policies.

To accomplish any of these goals, Biden will have to actually do something about the trade deficit, currency manipulation, and the strong dollar. A voluntary solution has been tried for decades, but negotiation hasn't worked because the countries know the United States will not enforce any agreements. Countervailing currency intervention—buying corresponding amounts of a foreign country's currency to make their currency rise in value—will not work because China and other countries block any purchase of their currency.

---

[5] Edited by C. Bergsten. 2016. "Time for a Plaza II in "International Monetary Cooperation," *Fred and Green Russell A*, p. 286–294, Columbia University Press.
[6] J. Ferry, Chief Economist. February 2019. "Imports Growth and Job Creation From a Competitive Dollar," *Coalition for a Prosperous America*, Working Paper.

Level playing field: When you look at Table 16.2, one wonders how did the United States ever allow all of our trading partners to impose tariffs and VATs against the United States over the last six decades, and did nothing to reciprocate. How did we ever allow the country to get into this jam? We are currently in an unsustainable game we cannot win, as long as we allow our trading partners to make us play on an uneven and unfair field. The time has come for strong enforcement and real penalties.

The United States has nothing to fear by getting tough on trade. We have tremendous leverage because all of these manipulating countries are export dependent, and we have the biggest consumer market in the world that everyone wants to sell to. They need us more than we need them.

Table 16.2 GATT *bound tariff rates with 25 countries*

All products, (S.A.%, 2021 UNCTAD)	
USA	3.4%
Japan	4.5%
European Union	4.9%
United Kingdom	6.0%
Canada	6.6%
Taiwan	6.8%
Switzerland	7.7%
Singapore	9.4%
Australia	9.7%
China	10.0%
Saudi Arabia	11.2%
UAE	14.6%
Korea	17.0%
Norway	20.1%
Israel	22.7%
Chile	25.2%
Philippines	25.7%
Thailand	28.0%
Turkey	28.9%
Peru	29.5%
Brazil	31.4%
Argentina	31.8%
Mexico	36.2%
Indonesia	37.1%
India	50.8%
Pakistan	60.9%

Source: Coalition for a prosperous America.[7]

---

[7] C. Benoit. March 22, 2012. "The GATT at 75: Look on My Works, Ye Mighty and Despair," Coalition for a Prosperous America.

The inconvenient truth is that we will never be able to grow our exports and stop the slow erosion of manufacturing as long as we allow currency manipulation and the dollar to be artificially inflated. We are slowly trading a way our future. I think if we lose the manufacturing sector, we will lose our economic soul.

CHAPTER 17

We Must Save America's Manufacturing Sector

Many economists believe that America will flourish in the postin-dustrial service economy. For instance, Lawrence Summers, who was chairman of the National Economic Council under President Obama, said, "there is no going back to the past where manufacturing was the dominant sector in the economy." He also said the new service economy would be built on "healthcare, retail, recreation, education, haircuts, insurance policies, hotels and homes." I think that Lawrence Summer's view, unfortunately, is the viewpoint of most American economists, and it has led to the deindustrialization of our economy.

In a 2016 article, *economics journalist Ben Casselman* said that Americans are nostalgic for manufacturing jobs, but they should stop asking for them, because they are not coming back. In fact, he said "talk a lot less about manufacturing period." He commented that it's time to start asking candidates how they plan to create well-paying jobs in the service industry.[1] This is a valid question because politicians and economists have ignored the fact that there are more low-quality service jobs than high-quality jobs being created.

We are now in the postindustrial service economy, but, as pointed out in Chapter 13, the service economy is not producing enough high-quality jobs and millions of workers are struggling. The idea that we could rely on services to replace manufacturing and maintain living standards was a fantasy. The WTO, International Trade Statistics show that manufactured

---

[1] B. Casselman. May 18, 2016. "Manufacturing Jobs Are Never Coming Back," *Thirty-Eight.*

goods account for 75 percent of world trade, and the export of services are beginning to erode because of the Internet and digitalization.[2]

I think that there is a general assumption by many economists that the erosion of American manufacturing is an acceptable premise in a changing economy. Just as the economy progressed from an agricultural economy in the early 20th century to an industrial manufacturing economy, it is now changing to a service economy. The assumption was that this transition is a healthy and natural process of economic evolution that allows resources to be deployed to new businesses with higher potential. Instead of a healthy process, it has become a large-scale experiment in deindustrialization and the assumption that the service economy will continue to prosper and maintain living standards is questionable.

But there is an even more important reason why the experiment of deindustrialization and manufacturing our technologies in foreign countries probably won't work out. That reason is the need for an innovation strategy that keeps America competitive in the global market place. Just as in the problem of climate change, depending on the deindustrialization experiment to continue without any controls could reach a point where America is no longer competitive and the situation is irreversible.

As Willy Shih and Gary Pisano argue in their book *Producing Prosperity*, "The combination of bad decisions by businesses and inadequate policies by government, is leading to an erosion of what we call America's Industrial Commons—the set of manufacturing and technical capabilities that support innovation across a broad range of industries." Their definition of the industrial commons includes knowledge and skills embedded in suppliers, skilled workers, and universities which are sources of competitiveness. It also includes infrastructure, research and development, process development skills and know-how, engineering, and manufacturing competencies related to specific technologies.

The purpose of their book is to "persuade business and government leaders to abandon the grand experiment of deindustrialization before it's too late." There are three important themes in their book:

---

[2] World Trade Organization. 2009. *International Trade Statistics* 62, p. 121. www.wto.org/english/res_e/statis_e/its 2009.htm

Theme 1: When a country loses its capability to manufacture, it loses the ability to innovate.

Theme 2: The key to economic growth is the industrial commons as defined earlier.

Theme 3: The erosion of the industrial commons was caused by government policy and decisions by the multinationals in outsourcing specific technologies.

Willy Shih and Gary Pisano's book focuses mostly on the high-technology products when they discuss the industrial commons, but I think there are some very traditional skills in manufacturing that are not mentioned and should also be a part of the industrial commons. They are forging and stamping, foundries, advanced machining, tool and die, and mold making. The tremendous loss of plants and jobs detailed in Chapter 6 reveals that a big part of these industries are now offshore, but we have also lost the skills, know-how, and operational competencies, and many of the skilled workers that make up their industrial commons. The material removal process in machining is fundamental to most industries and products, and the highly skilled artisans who make the jigs, fixtures, dies, molds, cutting tools, and gauges used in the manufacturing process are also ubiquitous to all manufacturing industries. They should also be included as part of our industrial commons because they are fundamental to the innovation process.

The Short- Versus Long-Term Problem

I have been watching outsourcing since the 1980s, and there seems to be a pattern in what happens to the industries and companies: A good example is the personal computer.

1. It begins with a U.S. corporation seeking a cost advantage and better short-term profits by outsourcing a product (or parts of a product) to a foreign country. In the 1980s, the creators of the personal computers decided to outsource the printed circuit boards to companies in Taiwan, South Korea, and China.
2. Once the corporation realizes the cost advantage, its competitors follow suit to try and stay competitive in the market. All of the

computer OEMs followed suit and began to outsource their circuit boards.

3. Along with the product, the critical knowledge, skills, tools, and process engineering also began to leave with the product, and the foreign manufacturers were free to find their own suppliers and sources of materials, eliminating U.S. suppliers from the supply chain. This was the beginning of the loss of the industrial commons.

4. After a time, foreign contractors were not satisfied with just making the parts and began to seek higher value-added work or a greater share of the total product and move toward complete product assembly and management of the whole supply chain. Eventually, the Asian contractors ended up making all of the Window's Notebooks, laptops, and other computers.

5. Once the foreign manufacturers had enough experience, they could do the design engineering and eventually didn't need the U.S. OEM. At this point, they take over the market and most of the original industrial commons are lost along with the technology.

So, in chasing short-term cost reductions and profits, the U.S. OEM inadvertently establishes the foreign supplier as a competitor and loses the market. This has happened with hundreds of products and markets originally invented by U.S. manufacturers. In focusing on short-term profits and shareholder value, they lose the long-term game.

Once the manufacturing of the product is outsourced, the commons are also lost because these skills and processes require daily interactions with manufacturing. According to Shih and Pisano,

> Without the ability to develop such new processes, they find they can no longer develop new products. In the long-term then, an economy that lacks an infrastructure for advanced process engineering and manufacturing will lose its ability to innovate.

This is perhaps the most important point of the book *Producing Prosperity*[3] because it throws cold water on the idea that America can

---

[3] G. Pisano and W. Shih. 2012. *Restoring Prosperity: Why America Needs a Manufacturing Renaissance* (Boston, MA: Harvard Business Review Press).

have a national strategy of innovation and at the same time, outsource manufacturing.

What happened to the personal computer is also happening today to the semiconductor, rechargeable battery, and solar cell industries. Our Asian competitors have gained so much of the manufacturing of these products that most of these U.S. manufacturers are now dependent on government subsidies or bailouts to survive in the United States.

More than any other business sector the U.S. multinationals were responsible for the erosion of the industrial commons. They outsourced all kinds of technologies and products with reckless abandon and with no regard for the skills and knowledge that would make America competitive in the future. It is puzzling to see how willing they were to allow their competitors to learn how to make some of these complex technologies knowing that one day they would have the power and the knowledge to dominate the world market and take the business away.

In his article "Who is Us?" Robert Reich makes the point that American MNCs have been moving abroad for decades and most have more employees overseas than in the United States. They now rely on their foreign facilities to do many of their most technologically complex activities, and they are exporting many of their products back to the United States.

Reich says,

> Apart from wartime or other national emergencies, American-owned companies are under no special obligation to serve national goals. Were American managers knowingly to sacrifice profits for the sake of presumed national goals, they would be acting without authority, on the basis of their own views of what such goals might be, and without accountability to shareholders or to the public.[4]

The American MNCs have become "stateless" entities with little or no loyalties to their home country. So probably trying to convince these corporations to stop outsourcing and to reshore their products would be an exercise in futility even though it would be in their long-term interest to do so.

---

[4] R. Reich. February 1990. *Who Is Us?*, Harvard Business Review.

What MNCS Could Do to Build the Commons Backup

However, corporations, both American and foreign owned, who still have their R&D, design, and manufacturing presence in the United States and still rely on American workers, are far more important to America's economic future than MNCs whose major investments are overseas. These companies could benefit from reestablishing the industrial commons because it will give them competitive advantage by establishing local capabilities.

Perhaps, the most compelling reason for rebuilding the commons is the commitment by 181 CEOs mentioned in the preface who signed a letter saying,

> The American dream is alive, but fraying. Major employers are investing in their workers and communities because they know it is the only way to be successful over the long term. These modernized principles reflect the business communities unwavering commitment to continue to push for an economy that serves all Americans.

So, for the managers of these corporations who must carry out this commitment, I suggest they consider:

> Do a careful analysis of their processes, knowledge, skills, tools, and the skilled people who build the products and use this information before committing to outsourcing.
> Develop a plan for long-term growth rather than on short-term profits and stock prices.
> If their long-term strategy is about competing with innovation, I suggest that if they want to compete in the USA, they remember that manufacturing and local R&D are intertwined with innovation.

How Can Government Help

Government, both Democratic and Republican administrations, are not viewed as helpful by the public. They seem to be lurching from crisis to crisis in a reactive mode often offering bailouts or subsidies after the manufacturing is established overseas as in the current semiconductor crisis.

The most helpful thing they could do to restore the industrial commons would be to develop an industrial policy that had specific goals and objectives. The plan should begin with a goal to reduce the trade deficit as well as an objective on increasing exports and a goal to increase manufacturing's share of GDP. Government could also help by establishing and funding apprentice training across a wide variety of manufacturing industries and to stop Chinese cheating by enforcing the rules of trade. They could also establish a list of technologies and products that are important to national security and make them off limits to all foreign competitors.

Federal Budget for Basic and Applied Research

Perhaps, even more important would be to increase the federal budget for basic and applied research, like we had in the 1950s and 1960s. The United States has a long history of investing in federal basic research going back to World War II, when federal research was used to develop radar, electronics, atomic power, jet fighters, and many other technologies used to win the war.

After the war, the United States continued to invest in basic science research, which was used to create many of the technologies and industries we see today. Federal basic research was the initial research used in developing the Google search engine, global positioning satellites, supercomputers, artificial intelligence, speech recognition, the Internet, smartphone technologies, the shale gas revolution, seismic imaging, LED light technology, magnetic resonance imaging (MRI), advanced prosthetics, and the human genome project. Many of these new technologies led to new industries spawning many new markets. An example that everybody understands is the Internet developed by ARPANET (advanced research products agency) of the Defense Department.

The development of new technologies into useful products was accomplished by private companies, but all of these products came, initially, from federal basic research in many fields of science. As an example, transistors were not suddenly discovered by the electronics industry; they came from people working with wave mechanics and solid-state physics. Light-emitting diode technology began with the study of infra-red emissions from gallium arsenide and other semiconductor alloys. Magnetic resonance imaging (MRI) came from research into spin echoes and free induction decay.

How Important Is Basic Research?

A study published in 2019 in the journal *Science* shows that one-third of all U.S. patents since 1970 relied on government-funded research. The study was based on an investigation of all patents issued from 1926 to 2017 and underscores the importance of funding basic federal research.

The Decline of Basic Research

According to the Information Technology and Innovation Foundation (ITIF), federal basic research has been declining for 22 out of 28 years. Figure 17.1 from the American Association for the Advancement of Science shows that as a percentage of GDP, federal research has fallen from a high of 1.3 percent in 1976 to 0.7 percent in 2018.

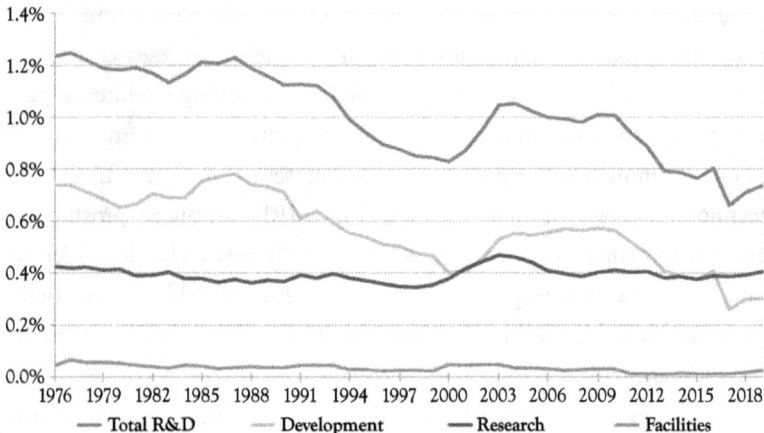

Figure 17.1 Business and federal R&D as a percentage of GDP

Note: Beginning in FY 2017, federal agencies have revised what they consider to be R&D. Late-stage development, testing, and evaluation programs, primarily within the Defense Department, are no longer counted as R&D. Based on AAAS analyses of historical OMB and agency data, R&D includes conduct of R&D and facilities.

The Five Reasons Maintaining a Manufacturing Sector Is Important

1.R&D and American innovation: Just about everybody from the conservative right to the liberal left believes that innovation is the primary strategy that America must depend on to compete in the global economy. President Obama, in a State of the Union speech, summed up our competitive challenge when he said, "The only durable strength we have—the only one that can withstand these gale winds—is innovation." He also said that "maintaining our leadership in research and technology is crucial to America's success."

But the loss of our technologies through partnerships, unfair trade, technology transfer, and espionage has shown that we are fast losing our technologies to countries like China. If we can't stop this ongoing loss of technology or halt the decline of the industrial commons, we will not be able to compete with a strategy of innovation.

If innovation is going to be the strategy that keeps America the Number 1 economy, then research and development is the key—and 68 percent of private R&D comes from manufacturing. The important point is that the majority of innovation and new technologies come from manufacturing—not the service industries. And, when a country loses its capability to manufacture, it loses the ability to innovate. Innovation and manufacturing are inextricably linked.

2. Advanced technology products: An analysis by the Brookings Institute defines 50 U.S. industries as ATIs. Thirty-five of the advanced industries are manufacturing industries, which make optoelectronics, nanotechnology, artificial intelligence, advanced robotics, advanced materials, self-driving cars, and weapons systems, to name just a few.

ATIs are very important to the American economy because they are our best shot at maintaining competitive advantage against foreign competitors—especially China. The ability to create these new technologies, particularly digital technologies, has implications for national security, economic growth, and the standard of living of most American citizens. In fact, this technological leadership is the key to economic power and remaining the largest economy in the world.

But as important as ATIs are, there are big problems emerging. America has been running trade deficits in advanced technologies since 2002. In 2020, the ATI deficit was $192 billion. The biggest ATI deficits are in information, communication, and telecommunications (ICT) ($270 billion). President Trump issued an executive order to secure the ICT supply chain because purchasing these products from foreign countries is considered a national security risk.

There are two significant reasons for ATI deficits.

1. Outsourcing production: American manufacturers do the R&D to invent these new technologies but then move the production to foreign countries to lower their production costs.
2. IP theft: China's primary strategy to get a hold of U.S. technology is to use joint-venture and technology-transfer agreements as a condition for companies to access Chinese markets.

Made in China 2025: At the same time as America is slipping competitively, China has launched an ambitious plan called "Made in China 2025." Under Chairman Xi Jinping, China has been open about the fact that they intend to seek dominance in many ATIs. The Made in China 2025 plan specifically targets information technology, biotechnology, flexible manufacturing (including robotics), advanced materials, aerospace, new energy vehicles, railroad technology, nuclear technology, and weapons. China knows that if they can acquire the technology without having to invest in the research and development, they can save a huge amount of time and money.

We need to stop the flow of these critical products and technologies to Asia and manufacture them in the United States if we are going to have a chance at developing an innovation strategy.

3. *Exports*: Manufacturing and exports were a top priority of the Obama administration, and the goal of the Obama administration was to double exports during Obama's second term. To attain this goal required increasing exports from $2,210,000,000 to $4,420,000,000 by 2016. But the U.S. economy fell well short of that goal, and the Obama administration did nothing to increase exports by reducing currency manipulation or the value of the dollar.

Exports as a percentage of GDP have been falling from 12.2 percent in 2012 to 10.2 percent in 2020 which does not bode well for the future of exports or any plan to reduce the trade deficit. In fact, we are beginning to lose our place as exporter to the world. China has taken over the Number 1 position in world exports. U.S. exports have fallen to Number 2 and Germany is Number 3 and likely to take over the Number 2 position. If increasing the ratio of exports to imports is the only way we can reduce our trade deficit, then manufacturing exports are not only vital they are the solution to the trade deficit problem.

In 2021, we exported $1.761 trillion and imported $2.851 trillion, for a trade deficit of $1.090 Trillion. Sixty-nine percent of our exports are manufactured goods—so if we are going to have any chance of reducing the trade deficit or increasing exports, the only answer is to increase manufacturing and decrease out sourcing. Services are only 27 percent of our exports, so increases of service exports simply won't do it. So, the obvious conclusion is that we will have no chance to reverse the trade deficit or employ a strategy of innovation if American manufacturing continues to decline.

4. *Manufacturing is key to our national defense*: An article in the *New York Times* by Peter Navarro made the case that the decline of the U.S. industrial base threatens national security. The article is based on a governmentwide assessment of America's manufacturing and military industrial base, identifying "almost 300 vulnerabilities, ranging from dependencies on foreign manufacturers to looming labor shortages."

Many industries, such as aerospace, high technology, software, and others, build the products that allow America to have the world's most powerful arsenal. Basic industries such as the chemical, petroleum, mining, and electronics industries are part of our strategic and defensive reserves. Maintaining these industries and the suppliers and skilled workers in them is a matter of national security.

Thirteen industries are declining that manufacture products and technologies critical to our defense, such as propellant chemicals, batteries, specialty metals, hard disk drives, flat panel displays, semiconductors, printed circuit boards, machine tools, and advanced materials. We can't have strong national security if we continue to outsource components and critical materials to low-cost countries. The only way to stop these critical products and technologies from falling into the hands of our competitors is for the government to declare some of them critical to national security and declare them off limits to foreigners.

5. *Manufacturing as the foundation of global power*: From the rise of England in the 19th century to the rise of America, Japan, and Germany in the 20th century and the rise of China, Taiwan, and Korea in the 21st century, manufacturing has been the key to the growth and power of each country. The power is not just building factories that manufacture goods; it is making the machinery that makes the goods. In my article, *Is US Manufacturing Losing Its Toolbox?*[5] I showed that machine shops, machine tools, forging, stamping, semiconductors, hand tools, and many machinery industries that are the tools of production are all declining. The primary point is that to remain a global power, America must have a strong manufacturing base.

From a strategic perspective, the manufacturing sector is more important than the service sector because it is:

- Vital to national security
- The only way to increase exports
- The creator of advanced technology products
- The foundation of any kind of innovation strategy
- The key to remaining a global power

No other sector in the economy can achieve these goals. If we want to remain the Number 1 economy in the world, we must do something about the trade deficit and restore the industrial commons. We won't maintain our position as the world's largest economy as a service economy.

The biggest opposition to any of these suggested solutions will be America's MNCs. Not all of them, but the big importers, Wall Street and corporations with plants in Asia, will want to maintain the status quo and they will lobby Congress hard (just like they did during the Dodd/Frank legislation).

---

[5] M. Collins. August 16, 2019. *Is U.S. Manufacturing Losing Its Toolbox*, *IndustryWeek*.

The fallacy of relying on the postindustrial service economy was best summarized by Harold Myerson in *The Washington Post*. He said:

"The Wall Street/Wal-Mart economy of the past several decades off-shored millions of factory jobs, which it offset by creating low-paying jobs in the service and retail sectors: extending credit to consumers so they could keep consuming despite their stagnating incomes; and fueling, until it collapsed, a boom in construction." He also writes that, "of all the lies that the American people have been told in the past four decades, the biggest one may be this: We'll all come out ahead in the shift from an industrial to post-industrial society. The post-industrial service economy turned out to be a bust. The time for neo-industrial America has arrived."[6]

I would add that continuing reliance on the postindustrial service economy might lead to a nation of software programmers and tattoo parlors looking for someone to invoice.

---

[6] H. Myerson. September 04, 2011. *The Fallacy of Post-Industrial Prosperity*, *The Washington Post*.

CHAPTER 18

Hope Is Not a Plan

The problems described in this chapter show that America is in economic decline largely because of the strategies used by MNCs for the last 40 years.

It has resulted in half of the working population struggling economically as the gap between rich and poor continues to widen. America's multinationals are most responsible for what has happened to the employees, communities, manufacturing, suppliers, and a good part of the middle class. Economists hoped that outsourcing would lead to cheaper imported products and rising living standards, but hope is not a plan and we need a comprehensive plan with an industrial strategy.

In 1989, I was in Washington, DC, and was doing research for my first book, *The Manufacturers Guide to Business Marketing.* During a visit to the Office of Technology Assessment, I found a newly published report called "Technology and the American Transition."[1] The predictions in this report turned out to be prophetic and an accurate prediction of what has happened in the last 50 years. Here are some of the predictions:

- During the next two decades, new technologies, rapid increases in foreign trade, and the tastes and values of a new generation of Americans are likely to reshape virtually every product, every service, and every job in the United States. These forces will shake the foundations of the most secure American businesses.

---

[1] J.H. Gibbons, Director. May 1988. *Technology and the American Economic Transition: Choices for the future,* Office of Technology Assessment.

- They will affect America's position in the world economy and the number and quality of jobs the American economy produces.
- Change can lead to wrenching dislocation and pain for workers with obsolete skills, for management unable to recognize opportunity, and for communities where traditional businesses have failed.
- Change can create an America in graceless decline—its living standards falling behind those of other world powers.
- Change can result in a growing gap between those fortunate enough to have the talents, education, and connections needed to seize emerging opportunities and those forced into narrowly defined, heavily monitored, temporary positions. This latter group could be forced to bear most of the costs of uncertainty.
- Another way of asking this question is whether people will be able to find a variety of attractive opportunities for work or whether only a credentialed elite will enjoy such opportunities.

All of these predictions have come true, but what the 1988 report did not predict was that America's multinational corporations (MNCs) would drive most of these predictions and be responsible for what happened to the employees, communities, manufacturing, suppliers, and a good part of the middle class. This book is a summary of what they did and how they did it.

From 1940 to 1980, We Reached the High Noon of the American Century

The New Deal and the period from 1940 to 1980 created a new form of capitalism that included all working people. I call it Democratic Capitalism. Democratic Capitalism created a new economic and political order where working people shared in the prosperity and their own productivity. During the period between 1940 and 1980, the United States experienced economic growth that built the middle class and launched the notion of the American Dream and upward mobility where every generation expected to exceed their parents.

America's MNCs were different in this period. They were focused on:

- Making high quality rather than cheap products.
- Investing in local economies, plants, and equipment.
- Training the best workforce which included apprentice training that led to journeyman status.
- Paying senior executive based on job performance rather than stock prices.
- Paying the CEO 58 times as much as the average employee rather than the ratio of 278 to 1 today.
- Supporting the local communities where their employees lived.
- Paying a 50 percent corporate tax rate rather than the 2017 tax rate of 21 percent.
- Contributing to the nation's welfare.
- And last on the list was shareholder value.

The Big Change

But after 1980, everything began to change. America's MNCs pursuit of low labor costs became the driving force that led to American manufacturing slowly moving offshore. After 1980, the new model for American manufacturers was to do the R&D, design, and marketing and to outsource the manufacturing of the product to low-cost countries. At the same time, the MNCs began to focus on shareholder value and short-term profits.

Academics and most economists supported outsourcing because they believed it would provide cheap products to consumers and that America could transition to a service economy that would provide good jobs and living standards to the middle class. However, after 40 years of outsourcing to low-cost countries, America has lost 7.5 million manufacturing jobs, lost many supply chains, closed 80,000 manufacturing establishments, destroyed many American towns and cities, and given our trade competitors our products and technologies. Outsourcing has bled America dry and helped all of our trading competitors to grow. According to the Coalition for a Prosperous Ameirca (CPA), between 2000 and 2019 American

Manufacturing lost 33.2 percent of its workers, who "suffered an average of 19.2% fall in their standard of living".[2]

America's goods trade deficit ballooned to more than $1 trillion in 2021. Proponents argue that it provides the most opportunities for both consumers and producers by creating more jobs and allowing competition to decide what businesses are successful. It has always been a mystery to me how so many economists can talk about the advantages of trade deficits and cheap imports, but never discuss the losers of the "big change." This notion of more jobs and opportunities has not worked out for much of the middle class.

In this chapter, I will show how the unfettered free market has shifted wealth and concentrated power in the top 10 percent at the expense of the bottom 90 percent. The gap between rich and poor has widened, and the new service jobs for workers with a high school education are low pay and low benefits, leaving millions of families in an economic struggle.

A key factor driving the changes in the economy was the concept of free market capitalism (FMC). This was a new type of capitalism based on the principles of the late economist Milton Friedman which basically supported anything the big corporations wanted to do within the limits of the laws which were changing fast because of deregulation. FMC minimizes government intervention and maximizes the role of the market. According to the theory of the free market, rational economic actors acting in their own self-interest and price goods and services the most efficiently. In Friedman's view, government regulations, trade barriers, and labor laws are generally thought to distort the market. Multinationals enthusiastically adopted the principles of FMC, and the following is a list of the primary changes and how they affected the economy.

1. *Winners and losers:* Robert Reich in his article

The Myth of the Free Market observes: If some people aren't paid enough to live on, the market has determined they aren't worth enough. If others rake in billions, they must be worth it. If mil-

---

[2] J. Ferry, Chief Economist. August 15, 2019. *Manufacturing Jobs and Income Decline,* Coalition for a Prosperous America.

lions of Americans remain unemployed or their paychecks are shrinking, or they work two or three part-time jobs with no idea what they will earn next month or next week, that's too bad; it's just the outcome of the market.[3]

Unfortunately, this sad statement is what happened to millions of workers.

2. *Outsourcing:* As a response to declining profits because of aggressive foreign competitors coming into their U.S. markets in the 1970s, American multinationals chose outsourcing as a primary strategy. Over the last four decades, MNCs decided that it was in the best interest of their shareholders to move jobs and production to low-cost foreign countries. Outsourcing took the form of reliance on foreign suppliers to manufacture components, the introduction of coproduction arrangements (joint ventures), and licensing technology including technology transfer agreements. It also began the slow hollowing of American industry.

   The paradox that is hard to understand is that allowing their competitors to get their technologies through technology transfer agreements and outsourcing is in the long term, self-defeating. Once the foreign manufacturer has enough experience by manufacturing the product, they can do the design engineering and eventually don't need the U.S. OEM and take over the market. So, in chasing short-term cost reductions and profits, the U.S. OEM inadvertently establishes the foreign supplier as a competitor and loses the market over the long term.

3. *Monopolies and oligopolies:* Capitalism is a free-market system that is supposed to promote competition because in classic capitalist theory, competition leads to innovation and more affordable prices for consumers. Without competition, a monopoly, oligopoly, or cartel may develop. Since 1980, capitalism, as practiced by U.S. MNCs, did not promote the ubiquity of competitive markets. On the contrary, it has been moving toward consolidation and oligopolies and now controls many markets, prices, and wages. I think it is in the DNA of

---

[3] R. Reich. September 16, 2013. *The Myth of the "Free Market" and How to Make the Economy Work for Us.*

capitalism to consolidate, and always attempt to control markets and pricing. Only the government can stop them, but there have been very few antitrust cases since 1980 and the multinationals enjoyed a target rich environment.

4. *The money gambit:* Another big change was the pursuit of profit at any cost, and there are many examples. The new mantra was short-term profit and shareholder value which led to reduction of labor costs, outsourcing, stock buybacks, and financial gambling rather than investment in tangible assets. A good example of the MNCs commitment was Mary Barra, CEO of General Motors, who summarized the situation very well when she said, "I want to assure our owners that we are focused on creating shareholder value." Increasing shareholder value for corporations turned out to be a strategy of increasing the stock price, reducing costs, increasing profitability, buying back shares of the company stock to make short-term profits; rather than investing in American plants and employees. Contrary to their public relation efforts to convince the publica they care about all stake holders, General Motors strategies have nothing to do with workers, families, communities, or the economies of states. It is all about shareholder value and short-term profit.

In their public commitment to make positive changes to support the Fraying American Dream, the multinationals didn't say if sacrificing profit would be part of their new strategies. If, in fact, they are unwilling to make any changes that reduce their profits than their whole commitment to change outlined in my Preface is simply a charade and a ploy to take credit for change to help their stakeholders when they really never intended to do anything that would lessen their profits.

5. *The rise of financialization and Wall Street:* Another good example of the money gambit is Wall Street whose primary goal has little to do with the creative work of establishing real assets through investment. Wall Street is doing distributive work of financial assets which is moving wealth from one source to another. Since 1980, the finance industry replaced manufacturing to become the largest sector of the U.S. economy, and the problem today is that Wall Street is only interested in Return On Net Assets (RONA) period. Investment in financial assets is crowding out investment in real

assets because the pressure is for quick returns and stock buybacks. The success of the finance industry is based on growing indebtedness and the use of financial engineering tools that redistributes wealth rather than creating new wealth. The big banks that are the heart of Wall Street are still too big to fail. America is now a debtor nation with a huge current account deficit, $54 trillion of debt, and a huge importer of foreign products. I think it is a house of cards that will crash again unless enough regulations can be introduced to change the Wall Street game. Left to their short-term profit strategies, inequality will worsen, manufacturing will not grow, GDP growth will remain low, and the potential for financial crashes will be high.

6. *Fair share of taxes:* The multinationals today are not paying their fair share of taxes. Since 1980, there have been five major tax cuts for the multinationals and their shareholders. The primary strategy used to convince the voters that tax reduction was good for everyone was "trickle-down economics" which theorized that the reduction of taxes on the wealthy would create more jobs and increase wages. Instead, it has led to rising inequality. The idea of lower taxes that lead to more jobs became so popular that despite recessions and the decline of the median income of the middle class, it is still regarded by conservatives as some kind of absolute truth. The tax cuts did not lead to more jobs and higher wages, but they have led to bigger federal deficits and less tax receipts to run the government.

7. *Domestic investment:* America's multinationals have been investing more in their foreign businesses than their domestic businesses. Research from the Roosevelt Institute shows that productive corporate investment disappeared in the last 30 years and has been replaced by shareholder payouts. They say, "Whereas firms once borrowed to invest and improve their long-term performance, they now borrow to enrich their investors in the short-run."

This problem is most obvious in semiconductor industry. Over the last four decades, U.S. chipmakers outsourced most of the manufacturing to foreign manufacturers in Taiwan, South Korea, and China to where only 12 percent of their production is made in the United States. The U.S. chipmakers spent far less of their profit on capital spending compared to their foreign competitors. So began the era of the "fabless chipmaker."[4] Most of their profits were returned to the shareholders and half went to stock buybacks. In 2021, the crunch came in the semiconductor industry, and these same chipmakers begged the government for $52 billion in bailout money.

8. *Stateless corporations:* In the last 40 years, America's flagship MNCs have slowly moved production and jobs overseas and are no longer American corporations. In his 1990 article "Who Is Us," Robert Reich argues that "the national identities of large corporations have become meaningless." Reich says,

The American MNCs have become 'stateless' entities with little or no loyalties to their home country. So, asking them to be loyal to America or to stop outsourcing production is probably an exercise in futility unless they see it as in their financial interests, or unless Congress passes laws making outsourcing less profitable.[5]

9. *Deindustrialization and free trade:* The decision to outsource also began the adoption of Free Trade Agreements (FTAs) and inadvertently began a national experiment in deindustrialization. Both Democratic and Republican administrations enthusiastically supported FTAs and ignored the problems caused by outsourcing manufacturing. This became a de facto decision to sacrifice manufacturing jobs and industries in order to import cheap consumer products. One must ask, how can something supported by most economists, and politicians said to make everybody better off, become so reviled by most of the public?

Free trade became a one-sided process where the benefits would flow to capital and the costs to labor. It is socialism for capital and free market for labor. For many working Americans, it has become a race to the bottom. The loss of manufacturing and the transition to a postindustrial service economy was acceptable to most econo-

---

[4] J. Ferry. March 30, 2021. *Absolutely Fabless Of Chips, Cash, and Supply Chains,* Coalition for a Prosperous America.

[5] R. Reich. February 1990. *Who Is Us?* Harvard Business Review.

mists and the government. But as Willy Shih and Gary Pisano said in their article on manufacturing, "the U.S. has been conducting a multidecade experiment testing the hypothesis that it can thrive as a postindustrial economy. American business leaders and policy makers must abandon that experiment now—before it is too late."[6]

Deindustrialization has led to sacrificing jobs, industries, technologies, suppliers, and communities, but it is based on hypocrisy. The big question is, Why should the workers in the lower and middle class be asked to do all of the sacrificing while the multinationals and their shareholders gain all the spoils?

The China Problem

On October 10, 2000, President Bill Clinton signed into law a historic bill granting Permanent Normal Trade Relations (PNTR) to China with the *hope* that China would become more democratic. China has ignored the agreement and exploited the United States using mercantilism, while our government chose to ignore China's cheating and not enforce the rules of the agreement. As investment in plants in China and Asia grew, MNCs accelerated outsourcing of jobs and production, and our trade deficit began to grow. The growth in America's trade deficit with China since 2001 has resulted in the loss of nearly four million domestic jobs—a quarter of which were in *California* and *Texas*.[7]

To make matters worse, China turned out to be a rogue trading partner controlled by the communist party whose reliance on methods of cheating we ignore at our peril. They are a mercantilist predator that plays by their own rules and have created a trading game that we are destined to lose. American multinationals are complicit in the China problem because they simply ignore China cheating to stay in the China market. Coca Cola told the Congressional Executive Commission on China (CECC) that "if they spoke up in any capacity about political prisoners

---

[6] G. Pisano and W. Shih. March 2012. *Does America Really Need Manufacturing?* Harvard Business Review.

[7] A. Soergel. January 30, 2020. "California and Texas Among Biggest Losers of Jobs From Growing China Trade deficit," *U.S. News.*

and human rights matters in Xinjian, they could lose market share in China." The MNCs in their pursuit of profit at any cost are willing to ignore China's military, surveillance state, and human rights abuses in exchange for market access and low costs.

Nancy Pelosi summarized the problem when she said

> If we do not speak out against human rights violations in China, we lose all moral authority to speak out against human rights violation anywhere. I would say to the business community as they demonstrate their cowardice … what worth is there in gaining market but losing your soul?

America is at a crossroads. *We must stop dealing with China as we hope they would be, and begin dealing with them as they are.* I think that sooner or later the United States will find China's mercantilist methods and human rights abuses intolerable, and we will have to decouple from them. I agree with Clyde Prestowitz in that we are in the beginning of a cold war with China and must defend ourselves, just as we did with the Soviet Union. Decoupling will be a long, slow, and contentious process, but it is time to face reality and do something for the country, our citizens, and American manufacturing. We need short-term sacrifice to avoid long-term collapse.

China shock: Our 21 years of China trade has led to an aftershock for many communities in the United States where the loss of jobs and plants has severely affected the local economies and has created economic deserts within our borders. Cities that have experienced plant closures and employment loss have suffered from declining housing prices and tax revenue, and the rise of poverty, alcohol and drug abuse, single parenthood, and many other social ills. Unlike many European countries, the United States does not have the social programs to help these communities, and ignoring the people who are facing new economic problems has led to the rise of populism and general unrest. This has resulted in long-term changes in the economy where millions will struggle.

A paper on "The Persistence of the China Shock,"[8] by David Autor and David Dorn, says that of 722 U.S. regions analyzed, 223 of them,

---

[8] D. Autor, D. Dorn, and G. Hanson. October 2021. "On the Persistence of the China Shock," NBER Working Paper 29401, p. 1.

or 32.8 percent, suffered absolute declines in real per capita income. This means that "the open door for Chinese imports reduced the incomes of one third of the U.S. public." They go on to say that "Trade with China is effectively a vehicle to transfer income from working class in the heartland to the affluent, who live mostly on both coasts."

A 2021 report on deindustrialization and white voter backlash, by Leonardo Baccini and Stephen Weymouth,[9] argues that deindustrialization threatens dominant group status, leading some white voters in affected localities to favor candidates they believe will address economic distress and defend racial hierarchy. The report shows that "whites associated manufacturing job losses with the loss of upward mobility and with a broader American Decline." As described in Chapter 3, I think that this problem is predominantly an economic problem facing white high school educated Americans who have been left behind in the new service economy. Many working Americans believe that upward mobility is no longer valid and the deck is stacked against the average citizen.

Hope Is Not a Plan

The rationale by many economists for outsourcing and trade deficits was the hope that cheap products from Asia would somehow maintain living standards. Economists "hoped" that the transition from a manufacturing to a service economy would provide the wages, living standards, and the economic growth in the postindustrial service economy. But it hasn't happened for millions of working people and hope is not a plan.

Zero sum game: A report from the Economic Policy Institute makes the argument that income redistribution in past decades is a zero-sum game, "with gains at the top coming right out of the pockets of the bottom 90 percent of Americans."[10] The report also argues that cutting top tax rates, deregulation of industries, and FTAs have accelerated inequality,

---

[9] L. Baccini, McGill University, S. Weymouth, Georgetown University. 2021. *Gone for Good: Deindustrialization, White Voter Backlash, and U.S. Presidential Voting,* American Political Science Review.

[10] J. Bivens. June 09, 2016. *Progressive Redistribution Without Guilt,* The Economic Policy Institute.

will not boost growth rates, and will continue to send a disproportionate share of income gains to the top 10 percent.

As the report on deindustrialization by Baccini and Weymouth argues, there is a strong sense in America today that something is seriously wrong in our economy, particularly for citizens with only a high school diploma. A host of indicators (see Chapter 3) show that the middle class is struggling and upward mobility is elusive. As a result of economic policy and strategy decisions in the last four decades, the traditional routes into the middle class have become more difficult to travel. Many workers are not earning enough to cover basic living expenses, and "a quarter of full-time working age adults are not earning enough money to meet economic needs like housing, utilities, food, health care, and transportation for themselves or their families." There is a new feeling by millions of Americans "that no amount of individual effort or self-improvement or thrift can guarantee a secure middle-class life." The American social contract—a promise of opportunity and security for those who act responsibly—is fundamentally broken.[11]

Many Americans now believe that the poor wage growth of American workers was a failure-by-design driven by the MNCs and their shareholders. As a result, wages have stagnated or fallen, while corporate profits and CEO salaries have reached new heights. According to Joseph Stiglitz, "In the U.S., the bottom 90% have endured income stagnation for a third of a century. Median income for full-time male workers is actually lower in real (inflation adjusted terms) than it was 42 years ago."[12]

Federal Basic and Applied Research: A report by the National Academies entitled "Rising Above the Gathering Storm, Revisited: Rapidly Approaching Category 5" assessed America's competitiveness in a rapidly evolving global economy. This sobering report asks, "how then is America to maintain, or preferably enhance, the future standard of living

---

[11] A. Traub and H. McGhee. June 06, 2013. "State of the American Dream: Economic Policy and the Future of the Middle Class, Testimony to the U.S. Senate Committee on Banking, Housing and Urban Affairs."

[12] J. Stiglitz. April 2003. *Globalization and Its New Discontents,* Norton and Company.

of its citizenry?" The answer (and seemingly the only answer) is through innovation.

But the "Gathering Storm" in the title means that the United States appears to be "on a course that will lead to a declining (not growing) standard of living for our children and grandchildren." To avoid this grim future, the report concludes that the only answer is "innovation through leading-edge research and world-class engineering."

Most politicians believe that the strategy that will keep America in the race and its position as global leader is innovation and the development of new technologies. But they don't seem to see that innovation comes from research and development and more than 70 percent of all private-sector R&D comes from manufacturing. The innovation strategy is in jeopardy for four reasons:

1. We are losing many of our latest technologies through outsourcing, joint ventures, and technology transfer agreements.
2. China needs America's latest technologies to be successful in their Made in China 2025 plan and will use both legal and illegal means to get them, unless we can stop them.
3. Basic and applied research by the federal government has been declining for many years. In the early 1960s, federal research spending was more than half of the total R&D spending; by 2012, it had fallen to 31 percent of total R&D. The decline of basic federal research is a very bad trend because this research is the lifeblood of all R&D, and most experts believe that declining basic research will eventually lead to declining GDP growth. In essence, cutting back on federal research is cutting back on R&D and innovation. This is truly a Gathering Storm that will have dire consequences to the nation, the economy, and working individuals.

Despite the attractiveness of the U.S. market, U.S. producers' market share is in decline. What's their market share like these days? The answer: 66.4%, based on the new Domestic Market Share Index (DMSI) created by Coalition for a Prosperous America (CPA) in July 2022. That means that nearly two-thirds of the manufactured goods made here are sold here currently. But it used to be 77.3% in 2002. The number is going in the wrong direction. Imports continue to replace domestic production no matter who is in the White House[13].

Our only chance of reversing the current situation and implementing a strategy of innovation will depend on American MNCs and the government. The government will have to limit access to the advanced technologies by our foreign competitors using national security restrictions or tariffs, and the multinationals will have to reduce outsourcing their technologies to their foreign competitors.

If the politicians are really serious about an innovation strategy, then the catalyst for jump starting an innovation renaissance is to increase federal basic and applied research. To fix the problem, we must convince Congress that it is vital to reinvest in federal research at 1965 levels, which means doubling the current federal research budget.

The McKinsey Global Institute has been a consultant to the MNCs for decades. The Coalition for a Prosperous American, in an April 2021 commentary, describes McKinsey as historically touting "open and free markets, big corporate power, and moving supply chains to scale up in Asia where labor was abundant and regulations were not." But now McKinsey has changed its tune to say that the United States is facing "a now-or-never moment to regain capabilities and market share. There is also a growing sense that its frayed social fabric will not be repaired without more middle-class jobs and attention to the places that have been left behind."

I think that McKinsey has reached a watershed moment where they see what is going to happen to our economy unless we make some real changes. Perhaps, the semiconductor industry (which has received a $52 billion bailout) has provided a lesson for what is going to happen to other declining U.S. industries and their MNCs.

After 1980, the interests of U.S. multinationals and interests of the country diverged. MNCs and Wall Street now have the nation by the throat and are dictating the future of the economy and living standards. What is good for them has turned out to be not good for employees,

---

[13] K. Rapoza. June 22, 2022. *American Manufacturer's Share Of Market Hits New Low*, Coalition for a Prosperous America, Weekly Recap.

American manufacturing, communities, or the country. The American Dream has been dismantled, and from the perspective of much of the middle class and supporters of American manufacturing, America is in decline. The big question is should America follow the economic path that the multinationals are following or commit to a different path that might serve more stakeholders and lead to better long-term outcomes?

In August 2019, 181 CEOs signed a commitment letter to lead their companies not just for the benefit of their investors, but "for the benefit of all stakeholders: customers, employees, suppliers, communities, and shareholders." They said they wanted to keep the American Dream alive. The only way, in my opinion, they can reach their new goals to help employees, communities, suppliers, and the country is to back away from their "shareholder-only" model and begin reshoring production, but so far, they are not walking their talk. Perhaps, the MNCs might be listening to what McKinsey is saying, or maybe, they are following the government bailout of the semiconductor industry and wondering if it might happen to them. We are at a "now-or-never moment."

This book describes the specific problems caused by America's MNCs to the country, their employees, their suppliers, and communities over the last 40 years. It is directed at the current and future managers of the MNCs in the hope that they will carefully evaluate the problems described in each chapter and consider enlightened solutions that will actually help all of the stakeholders described in their 2019 public commitment. If these corporate managers decide that it is not in the interest of the corporation to change their strategies and tactics, then the only alternative is to wait for things to get worse and rely on government to design legislation as solutions to these problems.

CHAPTER 19

Solutions

This chapter makes the essential point that just offering general goals and a general industrial policy seldom works. But to turn goals into a reality requires developing a plan with measurable objectives. The chapter lists 12 measurable objectives that offer solutions to the nation's many economic problems. It concludes with an appeal to the managers of the MNCs and how they might use this book to carry out their CEO's pledge to meeting the needs of all stakeholders, including employees, suppliers, communities, and an economy that serves all Americans.

America's industrial policy is based on free trade and outsourcing which has hollowed out the U.S. manufacturing base. Russia has invaded Ukraine and has made an agreement with China to oppose the United States in what they call "hegemony." Should this crisis intensify, the United States is too dependent on China and other foreign countries, for a wide range of products necessary for national security.

Developing an Industrial Policy and Plan

Debate about whether we need a national industrial policy is a false choice. We have a policy but our current policy leaves the nation lurching from crisis to crisis, and we never seem to come up with good solutions to long-term problems. As the shortages of medicines and PPE products revealed during the COVID-19 pandemic, we no longer have domestic sources for many products connected to national security, and, in fact, have lost control of many industries and technologies. It has become obvious that we need a new industrial policy and plan.

President Biden's Build Back Better Plan is a good example. It included general goals such as increasing manufacturing employment by five million jobs, strengthening unions, investing in infrastructure, and protecting supply chains and some industries. But to turn his goals into a reality, the President needs to develop a plan with measurable objectives. Without measurable objectives, nothing will change and we won't reindustrialize America.

The first compelling reason to develop a plan is that our competitors have industrial policies and manufacturing plans that have allowed them to successfully export to the United States. In fact, China's "Made in China 2025" plan spells out exactly which industries and technologies they want to dominate in the future. Why can't we develop a plan?

Second, the Bureau of Labor Statistics shows that 38 U.S. manufacturing industries continue to decline in terms of establishments and employment. We need a strategy to stop the erosion of our manufacturing base and specify which industries are critical and need to be saved.

Third, we need to prevent the loss of high value-added manufacturing sectors and the advanced technologies that will allow America to compete with a strategy of innovation on the world stage.

But before designing a plan with specific strategies, the government needs to first publicly commit, in writing, to saving American manufacturing by reducing the trade deficit. President Joe Biden has made a big deal out of his plan to "ensure the future is Made in America by America's Workers," and he wants to create manufacturing jobs and grow the manufacturing sector. But to achieve his goals, he will have to find ways to reduce the trade deficit by stopping currency manipulation and decreasing the value of the dollar.

All past administrations also began with lofty goals about growing manufacturing, but when it came time to do something to reduce the trade deficit devalue the dollar and stop currency manipulation, the Treasury Department always chose to keep the dollar strong and ignore currency manipulation. Subsequently nothing changed.

The government must get its act together, speak with one voice, and say exactly how they will bring back manufacturing. As long as the dollar is overvalued, and cheap import prices is the objective, there is no reason for American manufacturers to invest in the United States, and every reason to move their production to low-cost foreign countries.

Measurable Objectives

To make any plan work, there must be measurable objectives. Clear and measurable objectives would require the government to show how and when a commitment would be achieved (probably why politicians don't like measurable objectives and prefer to speak in generalities). The following objectives would help Biden move toward reindustrializing the country.

Objective 1: Five million new manufacturing jobs: The plan needs to say how many jobs per year for the next four years. Table 19.1 shows that it will take a reduction in the trade deficit of 20 percent to bring back one million manufacturing jobs. So, more importantly, the President needs to address the next three objectives to have any chance of success.

Objective 2: Trade deficit: On December 31, 2021, the United States passed $1 trillion in the goods trade deficit. You don't have to be an economist to reason that a country can't pile up debt faster than its income forever. In an article, "Americans Backing a Competitive Dollar," John Hansen says, "our debt to foreigners as a share of GDP has risen from 20 percent to about 70 percent last year." He says, "from 2017 to 2020 our net external debt grew 22.5 percent while our GDP grew at barely over one-tenth that rate—2.4% per year." John makes the argument that these trends are unsustainable and that "our net debt to foreigners would exceed 100% of GDP by 2023."

It is worth noting that politicians, Democrats or Republicans, don't seem to be willing to publicly commit to an objective of reducing the trade deficit, and they act as if we can continue to increase debt to foreigners without any economic repercussions forever. This is dangerous territory, and government is the only entity that can do anything about the trade deficit. I would be more of a believer in Biden's effort to create five million manufacturing jobs if he would publicly commit to an objective to reduce the trade deficit.

Objective 3: Currency manipulation: Any attempt to reduce the trade deficit must address currency manipulation and dollar valuation. So, the first step is for the treasury department to admit that 15 of our trading partners are unfairly manipulating currency and keeping the dollar value high so that our export prices are not competitive.

Most of the large importer corporations and Wall Street do not want the government to enforce the current WTO and IMF laws against currency manipulation or to devalue the dollar because they want to keep foreign import prices low. This keeps U.S. export prices artificially high and makes American products uncompetitive. It also grows our trade deficit.

The inconvenient truth is that we will never be able to grow our exports, stop the slow erosion of manufacturing, reshore jobs and production, and employ a policy of reindustrialization as long as we allow the dollar to be artificially inflated. In fact, I don't think it will be possible to achieve the growth rates we enjoyed before 1973 as long as we allow currency misalignment. Indeed, during his campaign for the Presidency, Joe Biden talked a lot about enforcement actions against China or any other country that was undercutting American manufacturing through unfair practices. But after he became President, his administration has sent mixed messages about currency manipulation and the dollar valuation.

In Biden's plan to ensure the "Future Is Made in All America" he pledged to "Take aggressive trade enforcement actions against China or any other country seeking to undercut American manufacturing through unfair practices, including currency manipulation." However, when asked about the dollar and currency manipulation, Biden's Treasury Secretary Janet Yellen said she believed "markets should set the value of currencies and that we would *not* seek a weaker currency to gain competitive advantage." She also said, the "United States should oppose attempts by other countries to artificially manipulate currency values to gain trade advantage." However, she didn't say how she would stop other countries from manipulating their currencies or how President Biden's pledge to create five million manufacturing jobs was going to succeed if she maintained a strong dollar policy. So, it looks like Biden and Janet Yellen will follow all previous administrations and avoid confronting the issues of currency manipulation and the strong dollar.

Objective 4: Dollar value: The root cause of the trade deficit is that the United States is not price competitive primarily because the dollar is overvalued by 20 to 30 percent. On June 8, 2021, the Biden administration issued Executive Order 14017 to improve America's supply chains. This order asked for a report on the information and communications technology sector, but it didn't address the cost problems caused by an overvalued dollar.

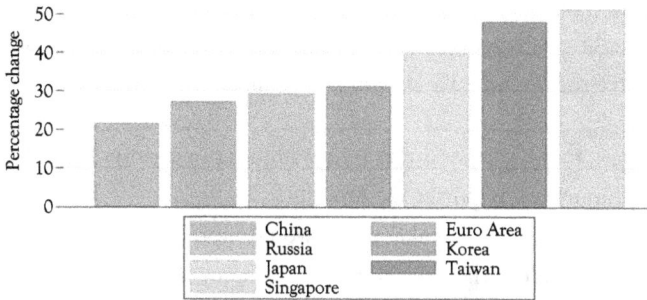

Figure 19.1 Exchange rate adjustments versus U.S. dollar required for current account balance

Source: Jeff Ferry, February 7, 2022, New Study: Global Currency Misalignment Challenges U.S. Reindustrialization Efforts, Coalition for a Prosperous America.

A study by the Coalition for a Prosperous America in February 2022 shows graphically why America is not competitive because of currency imbalances. Figure 19.1 shows the persistent dollar misalignment against seven countries. U.S. producers are trying to compete with these countries operating at a disadvantage of 20 to 40 percent, so the obvious conclusion is unless we can do something to reduce the value of the dollar, American efforts to reshore American production and increase exports are doomed are doomed to fail. The truth is that we will never be able to increase exports or reduce the slow erosion of manufacturing industries and technologies as long as our competitors are allowed to manipulate their currencies to keep the dollar overvalued.

What it gets down to is a titanic struggle between two completely different ideologies:

1. The big importers, Wall Street and the Treasury department who favor the strong dollar, trade deficits, and cheap imports,
2. Versus the supporters of domestic manufacturing, reshoring, exports who favor reindustrialization.

This is perhaps the quintessential argument of the book, so let me make it crystal clear.

Perhaps, the most influential representative of the strong dollar camp is Larry Summers who was Obama's Chairman of Economic Advisers. He offers three reasons why we should maintain a strong dollar:

- First, that a weaker dollar means higher priced imports and less purchasing power for Americans.
- Second, he feels a weaker dollar would mean higher interest rates.
- Third, there is the possibility of a currency war if other countries seek to weaken their currencies to remain competitive.

On the other hand, if we do nothing about the dollar:

- We will lose most of our manufacturing industries shown in Table 6.1 in Chapter 6.
- We will continue to lose our technologies shown in Figures 5.1 and 5.2 to our foreign competitors and eventually the markets.
- There will be no incentive for the MNCs to reduce outsourcing.
- With the loss of the industrial commons, technologies, and manufacturing, we will also reduce the R&D generated by the manufacturing sector, and we won't be able to compete using a strategy of innovation.
- Exports will never exceed value of imports because 70 percent of exports are manufactured goods.
- The goods trade deficit was $1.07 trillion in 2021 and will continue to grow.

Contrary to Mr. Summers argument for cheap imports and more purchasing power for consumers, if you look at Tables 3.1 to 3.4 in Chapter 3 the cheap imports theory doesn't seem to be working for much of the middle class. In a 2018 oped article, Summers said "Beyond style, there are good economic reasons why the last 7 Treasury Secretaries stayed with a strong dollar mantra."[1] He doesn't expand on this assertion, but I think the primary reason that all treasury secretaries are for the strong dollar

---

[1] L.H. Summers. January 25, 2018. "Why Treasury Secretaries Should Stick With the Strong Dollar Mantra," Mossavar-Rahmani Center for Business and Government, Blog.

is that they come from the financial industry and the financial industry makes the most profit when the dollar is strong. The essence of their argument is that they are willing to throw nonfinancial industries under the bus to maintain a strong dollar.

Continuing to support the strong dollar is an ongoing commitment to deindustrialization and ever-increasing debt. I think the most compelling argument came from Michael Pettis in his book *The Great Reckoning*. He said "Any policy that does not clearly result in a reversal of the deep debt, trade and capital imbalances of the past decade is a policy that cannot be sustained."

My argument is that the imports of cheap products don't seem to be helping most of the middle class, and if we look at the longer term and how America can remain competitive, I don't see any alternative but to steadily reduce the value of the U.S. dollar, and there are many tools the government can use to achieve the objective. If President Biden really wants to achieve his objective of adding five million manufacturing jobs, Table 19.1 shows he would have to reduce the trade deficit by 30 percent by reducing the value of the dollar and stopping currency manipulation.

Similar steps were taken between 1985 and 1987 by the Reagan administration called the Plaza Accords, the last major period of dollar revaluation, and they worked. The treasury department should state a measurable objective on how and when they can reduce the value of the dollar per year. The following are four different methods that can be employed for dollar revaluation:

- *Countervailing duties* (CVDs): These are tariffs or taxes on imported goods that offset subsidies by our various trading partners. CVDs could be in the form of a surcharge, tax, or tariff. Even though tariffs have hurt some importers, there is proof that they have really helped U.S. manufacturing.
- Taxing purchases: Using a *market access charge* for all foreign investors buying U.S. assets would begin to lower the value of the dollar to a trade balancing price. The plan would require the federal reserve to impose a "market access charge" on foreign investments in the United States. This tax would cover asset purchases including stocks, bonds, real estate, or intellec-

tual property—pretty much everything foreigners might want to buy, except for goods to be exported. The stated objective is to achieve a *current account balance* within five years.

- Implementing a *withholding tax* on the profits and dividends earned by foreign investors that finance the dollar.
- *Taxing sellbacks*: Biden has proposed a 30 percent tax on the profits of companies that have offshored, but, so far, Congress has not approved his proposal.

Objective 5: Reshoring manufacturing: In 2021, 1,334 companies reshored 138,110 jobs, but at the current rate of reshoring, it will take over 30 years to reach Biden's goal of five million jobs. Companies offshore because they can buy many products offshore for 30 percent, even 50 percent, less. The most direct approach is to devalue the dollar. But the reality is that the big importers, Wall Street and the Treasury department who favor the strong dollar, are a powerful lobby, and it simply may not be politically feasible to devalue the dollar.

An alternate strategy for reshoring has been proposed by Harry Moser, founder of the Reshoring Initiative. He developed a simple chart that quantifies the competitiveness gap that shows how incremental reductions in U.S. products' prices would lead to reshoring manufacturing jobs.

Table 19.1 shows that a 20 percent reduction in the trade deficit will result in one million jobs being reshored. But, column 3 shows that the U.S. price would have to be reduced by 10 percent versus offshore prices to achieve the objective. The U.S. price would have to be reduced by 30 percent to achieve 100 percent of trade deficit reduction.

Table 19.1 Manufacturing jobs/price matrix

Desired trade deficit % Reduction	Number of Mfg. jobs Brought Back	Required U.S. price vs. import Required	Time to steady state
20%	1 million	10%	10 years
40%	2 million	15%	15 years
60%	3 million	20%	20 years
80%	4 million	25%	25 years
100%	5 million	30%	30 years

Source: Harry Moser, Reshoring Initiative, March 12, 2021.

Table 19.2 *Competitiveness toolkit*

Competitiveness toolkit: factors and impact					
Factor	Model	Δ Price advantage	Time to implement years	Ease of passage, 1–10, 10 high	Severity of secondary impacts, e.g. inflation
Skilled work-force	Germany and Switzerland	5%?	10–20	8	
15% Corp. tax rate	Ireland	2%	1	5	
15% VAT	Most of the world	15%?	1	2	
$ Down 20%	Most of the world	7%?	3	5	
Less regulations	?	3%?	5	4	
Healthcare costs down 30%	Germany	3%	15	2	
Universal use of TCO and CDF for sourcing and sitting decisions		10%	4	4	
Make duty rates reciprocal		3%	3	5	
Innovation					
Automation					
?					
Total		48%			

Harry's alternative solution to dollar devaluation is to aggressively reduce manufacturing costs by using a range of policies in his Competitiveness toolkit (Table 19.2). His overview is as follows:

1. Level the playing field: Create a vetted national policy tool to select the optimal actions that will bring back the desired number of manufacturing jobs with the least collateral damage. The actions will also keep jobs from leaving and increase exports.
2. Overcome the wide belief that the United States cannot and will never again produce many of the products that have been lost to offshoring. Show that there is a path to adding millions of manufacturing jobs.
3. Advance from the current condition, many groups proposing, but not quantifying their solutions impacts, to a unified, quantified proposal for the nation.

Most importation of manufactured goods is, finally, motivated by price, that is, by lower wages and manufacturing costs abroad. Harry's key to reshoring is his Competitiveness toolkit (Figure 9.2) which lists eight factors that are strong candidates for achieving cost reduction. The 3rd column is his estimate of the potential price advantage, and the 4th column is the time to implement in years. Finally, he rates the chances of success in a scale of 1 to 10.

He asks American manufacturers, Non Governmental Organization (NGOs), and government offices to refine the estimates presented in the table, to add additional factors, and to share with Harry at info@reshorenow.org to create a unified proposal. The Competitiveness toolkit is a very pragmatic solution to cost reduction and the trade deficit.

If dollar devaluation is not politically acceptable, Harry's broad approach will enable American manufacturers to compete against aggressive foreign countries who have lower wage rates achieved in part by manipulating their currencies.

Objective 6: Critical industries: There are 38 manufacturing industries shown in Table 6.1 in Chapter 6 that are declining in terms of lost factories and jobs, so the plan needs to say which of these industries we are willing to save. It should also say which of the Advanced Technology Products (ATIs) should be protected.

Objective 7: GDP percentage: Manufacturing was 21 percent of GDP in 1975 but has been slowly eroding for years. It is now 10.8 percent of GDP. The plan should state the objective for what the GDP percentage should be in five years. If we can make headway in most of these objectives, a reasonable objective would be 16 percent of GDP.

Objective 8: Exports: Increasing our exports is a critical factor in balancing trade. It should not be a general goal like Obama's 2010 goal of doubling exports. We need a measurable objective that is connected to the dollar devaluation and can be measured year to year in terms of percentage increases in exports. A new working paper from the CPA called "Imports Growth and Job Creation from a Competitive Dollar" reveals that if the dollar value could be reduced by 27 percent it would result in export growth five times faster than baseline, while imports would grow more slowly.

Objective 9: Imports: Closely allied to exports, a reduction in imports would also help to attain the objective of reducing the trade deficit and can be measured year to year in terms of % decreases.

Objective 10: Make China tariffs permanent: The Trump tariffs with China are working, and, in fact, are our only defence against China's mercantilist cheating. We need to continue to use them to slow the flood of cheap imports and move toward a balanced trade budget.

The Section 301 tariffs are the best leverage the United States has in negotiating with China. Weakening them takes away any chance we have for stopping China cheating, particularly IP theft. The Coalition for a Prosperous America said, "The Section 301 tariffs were primarily a punishment for China's IP theft, though not every item targeted under the tariffs relates to intellectual property. For this reason, exclusions were given in the first year to importer companies who had convinced the trade ambassador to remove tariffs on their imports." There is growing pressure in Congress to extend the exclusions. The multinational importers have had four years to find other sources for their imports. Hundreds of them have not and they are relying on Congress to either get rid of the Section 301 tariffs or to grant more exclusions.

Congress should limit tariff exclusions for importers, especially those that are not using the imports to manufacture in the United States. In addition, the United States should implement the full Section 301 duties on the list four items that are valued at $300 billion.

Objective 11: Research and development: According to the Information Technology and Innovation Foundation (ITIF), federal basic research has been declining for 22 out of 28 years. It is difficult to see the positive outcomes of an investment in basic research because it does not lead to visible products in the short term. But in the long term, disinvestment can lead to stagnant productivity, lagging competitiveness, and reduced innovation. To maintain our role as the innovation leader in the future, the Biden plan to Ensure the Future Is Made in All of America asked Congress for $300 billion over four years. The ITIF thinks the United States needs to increase federal research to 2.0 percent of GDP or about $450 billion per year (Figure 19.2).

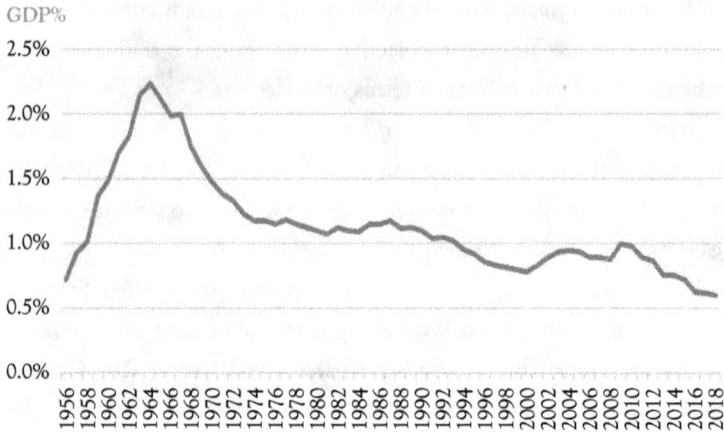

Figure 19.2 Federal R&D as a share of GDP

Source: October 4, 2021, Congressional Research Service, U.S. Research and Development Funding and Performance: Fact Sheet, Figure 2 Federal and Business Shares of U.S. R&D Expenditures, 1955 to 2019.

Objective 12: No new trade agreements: There will be pressure from multinationals to revise the Trans-Pacific Partnership (TPP) agreement during the Biden Presidency. A government report by the International Trade Commission (ITC) in June 2021 analyzing the results of 16 FTAs from 1985 to 2020 showed that there was very little growth or job creation and most of the economic benefits went to the multinationals and their investors. FTAs were good for white-collar but not for blue-collar workers and were good for big corporations like General Motors but not small or midsize supplier firms. We should oppose any FTA that will lose jobs or increase the trade deficit.

Even though reindustrialization and saving American manufacturing are vital to the future of the country, I must also admit that there are many people against having a plan or any industrial policy because they want to maintain the status quo. At the top of the list are the big box retailers, Wall Street, and corporations which have invested in plants in China and Asia to ship their products back to the United States. They will be very resistant to any changes that restrict imports or reduces the value of the dollar, but it is really in their interest to evaluate the bigger picture and face up to the fact that they are slowly losing their competitiveness by outsourcing and allowing their competitors to get their technologies.

America is a country lurching from crisis to crisis without a plan or even a clear direction.

Level Playing Field

One of the big questions about American trade policy that has always puzzled me is why do we think it would be good for America to allow all of our trading partners cheap access to all of our industries when they won't give us the same access to their industries? A good example is the automobile industry. According to former U.S. Secretary of Commerce Wilbur Ross, "The EU charges a 10% tariff on imported American cars, while the U.S. imposes a 2.5% tariff on imported European cars. Europe exports four times as many cars to the U.S., or 1.14 million cars per year."

If the objective is to create a more a level playing field with our trade partners, we need to build reciprocity into our trade. The former trade negotiator, Peter Navarro, urged Congress to pass a Reciprocal Trade Act, which would allow the United States to impose reciprocal duties on all countries who have higher tariffs if they do not lower their tariffs and VATs. This is a pragmatic solution because all of our trading partners have tariffs and VATs that range from 9.2 to 26.9 percent. We are currently in an unsustainable game we cannot win, as long as we allow our trading partners to make us play on an uneven and unfair field. I think the time has come to play a reciprocal trading game. Why not reciprocate tariffs and VATs in order to get our trading partners to reduce theirs?

We need to take a hard look at Germany. Despite China, they still have a very strong manufacturing sector even though their wages are high, they have strong unions, and labor has a place on their corporate boards. Their savings rate is 11 percent compared to the United States's 2.9 percent of GDP, and their health care costs are half of what we pay in the United States. Their version of free trade is very protectionist, and they have a 19 percent value add tax with tariffs averaging 5.1 percent. Their manufacturing sector was 18.1 percent of GDP compared to the United States's 10.8 percent of GDP in 2020. We need to examine how Germany plays the international trade game and abandon our historical open markets approach to free trade.

Leaving the WTO

In his book, *The World Turned Upside Down*, Clyde Prestowitz says that the WTO was supposed to lead to better trade rules and more order, but it failed for several reasons. It has ignored currency manipulation, trade imbalances, and IP theft. Second, it has failed in effective governance because the 164 member countries must make decisions by consensus. And, it has completely failed at controlling China's mercantilism including State Owned Enterprises (SOEs), subsidies, market protections, IP theft, and so on.

The 164 members making decisions by consensus has turned out to be detrimental to the United States. All of the member countries want to export to the United States because we have the biggest consumer market, the lowest tariffs, and no Value Added Taxes (VAT). The WTO members will always vote against any effort by the United States to level the playing field.

The WTO has rendered itself ineffective and can no longer assure free trade, particularly with China. Prestowitz goes on to say, "The WTO simply has no way for dealing with politically guided and coercive trade, investment, and industrial politics, any more than the IMF can deal with issues of chronic undervaluation and overvaluation of currencies and chronic trade surpluses." He suggests that "In view of this situation, the United States must lead the establishment of a new body, a democratic globalization organization," and its "members would include only democratic governments operating under the rule of law."[2]

Clyde Prestowitz suggests that the United States should leave the WTO and form a democratic globalization organization whose members are only democratic governments. The key members would be the United States, Canada, Mexico, the EU, United Kingdom, Japan, South Korea, Australia, India, Brazil, South Africa, and Nigeria. It would make decisions based on weighted voting, where the larger economies would have more weight in voting. The focus of the organization would be to aim for balanced trade with no member having chronic deficits or surpluses.

---

[2] C. Prestowitz. 2021. "The World Turned Upside Down, America, China, and the Struggle for Global Leadership," *Yale University Press*, pp. 268–269.

I think this is a very reasonable suggestion, because the WTO is not supportive of the United States, and has done almost nothing to stop China's mercantilism. Plus, there is growing anti-WTO sentiment in Congress.

Decoupling From China

With no trade organization that can protect the United States from Chinese mercantilism, the only practical alternative is to begin the process of decoupling from China. The original rationalization for allowing China into the WTO was that it would move China to become a more democratic country with an open market. The policy makers assumed that working interdependently with China would bring greater stability because both countries would be more dependent on each other's fortunes. China would then become cooperative and more honest trading partner and a reasonable competitor.

But it simply did not happen. Instead of becoming more democratic, China under Chairman Xi has intensified the Communist Party's totalitarian power over its people and is now a big threat to Hong Kong and Taiwan.

FBI Director Christopher Wray said Chinese IP theft in 2021 reached a new level

> more brazen, more damaging than ever before, and it is vital that we all focus on that threat together. Whatever makes industry tick. They target source code from software companies, engineering designs from manufacturers, testing data and chemical designs from pharma firms, personal data from hospitals and credit bureaus and banks.

Neil Jenkins from Cyber Threat Alliance told the committee that China's "Made in China 2025 Plan was a useful guide to the industries that China will target for intellectual property theft which includes information technology, robotics, aerospace, biopharmaceuticals, medical, electrical, farming, rail, new energy vehicles, and green technologies."

We now know from experience that China will use every method at their disposal (legal or illegal) to get their hands on these technologies so they don't have to invest in R&D. We also know that U.S. multinationals will continue to let them access our technologies through tech transfer agreements.

After decades of our government and U.S. MNCs advocating the outsourcing of American products and jobs—and touting the advantages of importing cheap Chinese products—it is time to face up to the fact that China is not going to change their predatory mercantilist methods, and they will eventually strip the U.S. multinationals of the technologies they need to compete in the future. Negotiation and agreements have never worked and so the next move is up to us.

In a blog on December 23, 2019, David Lynn summarized the China situation succinctly when he said,

> China has been a bad actor and economic predator for decades and gotten away with just about everything with respect to America and global trade. It has consistently lied about and reneged on every agreement and reform it promised to implement.

The decoupling process has already begun with Trump's tariffs, which should be made permanent. Support for decoupling has also started in Congress with Republican Senators like Josh Hawley, Tom Cotton, and Marco Rubio and Democratic Senators Tammy Baldwin and Mark Warner.

After the invasion of Ukraine by Russia, there is a movement to get the United States onto "wartime footing," which, hopefully, begins with repealing the Permanent Normalized Trade Relations (PNTR) with both Russia and China. We need a plan that shows how we can systematically decouple from China and rebuild domestic manufacturing industries so that we can become self-sufficient in critical minerals, and high-tech components needed for national security. The process should start by assessing our vulnerabilities and declare which industries and technologies are both critical and vital to national security. The plan must also explain exactly how we will:

- Make existing tariffs permanent including the 4A and 4B lists valued at $280 billion. List 4B covers 538 categories worth approximately $160 billion in imports. List 4A covers

3,207 product categories worth approximately $120 billion in imports. As part of the negotiation for the Phase One agreement, the U.S. Trade Negotiator suspended the implementation of the 4A and 4B and imposed a 25 percent tariff on lists 1, 2, and 3 worth approximately $240 billion.[3] But the time has now come to impose the 4A and 4B tariffs.

- Use the Defense Production Act to help American manufacturers begin to reshore production that is related to national security with federal guarantees of purchases.
- Use the Federal Financing Bank to fund the rebuilding of domestic industries.
- Expand the blacklist of all Chinese companies that continue to cheat and use the customs agency to prevent their products from being imported to the United States.
- Declare a list of technologies and products necessary for our national security and describe how they will be protected, particularly our advanced technologies.
- Describe incentives for American corporations to reshore their production or find better foreign vendors.
- Assess fines on all SOEs that are subsidized by the Chinese government and not allow them to compete in the American economy as long as they are subsidized.
- Stop China from accessing American university research labs or contracting with American scientists on work that affects our national security.
- Stop any future forced technology transfer agreements by American companies manufacturing in China if the technology has national security implications.
- Audit the 156 Chinese corporations (as of 2020) listed on the NYSE, Nasdaq, and NYSE. If they won't submit to an audit, then they should be removed from the stock exchanges for withholding information from their investors.

---

[3] N. Iacovella. February 2, 2022. "CPA Calls for Full 301 Tariff Implementation in Light of China's Violation of Phase One Deal," *Coalition for a Prosperous America.*

It goes without saying that many American corporations will probably oppose decoupling, but they are going to be pressured to change because the politics and public opinion regarding China are changing in the United States. I think they might cooperate if the government can give them some relief from forced technology transfer and some protection of their products and markets. Big-box retailers like Walmart and Target source many of their products from China and will not want to upset their supply chains. But if the tariffs on the consumer products become permanent, they may not have any choice but to pass on their prices or find new foreign vendors.

On February 24, 2022, Michael Stumo, President of the Coalition for a Prosperous America, said,

> The American people already know that our nation is overly dependent on China. But the stark realities of a new war make clear that Washington can't drag its feet another minute. For our nation's safety and security, we must start decoupling from China right now—and rebuild the industries that can make the United States more self-reliant in a hostile world.

Technology Transfer and Intellectual Property Theft

Former President Trump railed against IP theft, but other than his tariffs, he did very little to stop Chinese acquisitions of our technologies. Both Democrats and Republicans whine about IP theft but say nothing about the MNCs agreeing to forced technology transfer agreements or outsourcing their new technologies to foreign manufacturers. We probably can't do anything about technologies that are already being manufactured in Asia, but the Congress can assemble a list of all technologies that affect national security and put them on a black list. The list should also include technologies that are part of the Made in China 2025 plan, to make it at least difficult for them to get their hands on the new technologies they need.

One idea is to replace the indiscriminate tariffs implemented by the Trump administration with carefully targeted sanctions imposed on the Chinese entities directly involved in technology misappropriation.

Of course, the question is will U.S. multinationals cooperate with the government? Probably not for technologies that are already outsourced, but they might be interested in protecting new technologies, because there is now abundant evidence that over the long-term, transferring their technologies and manufacturing to foreign countries is a game, they won't win against unscrupulous countries like China who are dedicated to taking our technologies and replacing us as the world's superpower.

Increasing Government Revenue

Politicians and economists, both liberal and conservative, seem to be ignoring the growth of federal deficits. According to the Manhattan Institute, "simply continuing current policies with modest interest rates would produce debt of nearly 200 percent of the economy within three decades—at which point, interest payments would consume 42 percent of all federal tax revenues".[4] (What ever happened to Ross Perot when we need him most.) When you couple this fact with major trust funds like Social Security, Medicare, and the highway fund that will run out of money, it becomes obvious that the government is going to need more revenue.

To have any chance of competing in the world economy and implementing any of the solutions in this chapter, the U.S. government is going to have to increase government revenue—which means an increase in taxes. Since 1981, the multinationals have had five generous tax reductions which have seriously reduced government revenue and increased the federal deficit. To get onto a path of sustainability, the government must get additional revenue.

The multinationals have enjoyed multiple tax breaks where they saw corporate taxes reduced from 50 to 21 percent, and the top 5 percent of income earners got tax rate reduction from 70 to 21 percent. This isn't going to be easy because the multinationals spend millions of dollars every year lobbying Congress to protect their tax avoidance strategies.

President Biden wants a pro-growth, progressive tax code. His plan as part of the Build Back Better Bill was to raise nearly $4 trillion in additional revenue over a decade. According to the Tax Policy Center, "The highest-income 20% of households (who make about $170,000 or more) would bear nearly 93% of the burden Biden's proposed tax increase, and the top 1% nearly three-quarters."

---

[4] B. Ried. February 12, 2020. *Why Deficits Still Matter*, The Manhattan Institute.

But the Build Back Better Bill was never approved by Congress, and we still need to increase government revenue. The fact remains that to have any chance to implement the solutions in this chapter or to get the United States off the path of increasing debt will require increasing government revenue. Here are some suggestions that will probably be acceptable to everyone except the multinationals and the top 5 percent of income earners.

1. Implement a Value Added Tax (VAT): Every one of our trading partners uses VATs. It is like a sales tax that is rebated on their exports. The way it works is that when the U.S. exports to other countries, that country adds a VAT to our export price, which inhibits the sales of our exports. We should level the playing field by introducing a program to match the foreign country's VAT which might encourage them to reduce or drop their VAT on U.S. exports.

2. Sales factor apportionment: This method would tax profits based on where the product is sold and eliminate the ability of multinational companies avoiding taxes by shifting profits offshore. "The analysis also found that by replacing the current corporate tax system with an SFA a system at 21 percent, the United States could earn an additional $97.8 billion in federal corporate tax receipts."[5]

3. Global Minimum Corporate Tax of 15 *percent:* Another proposed bill would give government the ability to tax our home company's overseas profits at 15 percent, and deter them from using tax shelter countries to avoid taxes. President Biden's Inflation Reduction Act, was passed by the Congress in 2022, and included a minimum 15 percent tax for corporations.

4. Claw back: President Biden pledged to establish a "claw back" provision to force a company to return public and tax benefits when they close down jobs here and send them overseas. This is part of an effort to eliminate tax benefits for outsourcing, but, so far, this provision has not been implemented.

---

[5] K. Rapoza. September 24, 2020. "Why Berkshire Hathaway, Apple, Disney Lead List of S&P 500 Companies Paying Under 10% in Taxes," *Coalition for a Prosperous America.*

5. Raising corporate taxes: Over the past 50 years, the share of tax revenue coming to the federal government from business has collapsed. According to a 2019 Gallup poll, about 7 of 10 Americans believe corporations are not *paying their fair share* in federal taxes. The reality: the federal government collected about $230 billion in corporate taxes in 2019, about 6.5 percent of federal revenues in 2019.

The 2017 Tax Cut and Jobs Act lowered corporate taxes from 35 to 21 percent. An investigation by the Coalition for a Prosperous America found that an analysis in 2019 of the S&P 500 companies showed they paid on average less than 9 percent in cash federal tax,[6] well below the new rate of 21 percent. Biden wants to raise the corporate tax rate from 21 percent back to 26.5 percent, but because the MNCs never pay the minimum tax rate, I see no reason why MNCs shouldn't pay 35 percent again.

According to the *Office of Management and Budget*, Corporate tax revenue accounted for 32.1 percent of federal revenue in 1952, but by 2012, the share of corporate tax revenue had fallen to 9.9 percent.[7] Perhaps, we could make exceptions for U.S. corporations who don't outsource and are focused on Biden's Made in America plan. But the stateless multinationals who are investing overseas and focused on stock buybacks should have to pay 35 percent.

6. Stock buybacks: This is a critical issue because MNCs are investing in stock buybacks rather than in physical assets that lead to long-term growth in America. The right answer is to make stock buybacks illegal like they did during the New Deal. But if this is fiercely resisted by the MNCs, then a heavy tax should be placed on every stock buyback transaction so that the government could at least gain some tax revenue from stock buybacks. A one percent excise tax on stock buybacks, was part of the Inflation Reduction Act and was passed. In 2021 stock buybacks reached $882 billion.

---

[6] Ibid.

[7] U.S. Office of Management and Budget. 2012. *Fiscal Year 2013 Budget, Historical Tables, 1934-2017 (Table 2.2)*. www.whitehouse.gov/omb/budget/Historicals

7. Taxes on the top 5 percent: Over the last 70 years, the wealthiest Americans have gone from paying the highest taxes to paying the lowest. In the 1950s, they paid 30 to 70 percent of their income in taxes. Today, they pay 21 to 28 percent. The fact that the very wealthiest people in America are paying the same rate as people down in the tenth percentile is outrageous and I think that individual tax rates for the top 5 percent of earners need to be raised to 50 percent.

8. No tax breaks for outsourcing: On March 11, 2021, U.S. Senators Chris Van Hollen (D-MD), Sheldon Whitehouse (D-RI), and Dick Durbin (D-IL) and Congressman Lloyd Doggett (D-TX) joined by over 100 House members, introduced the No Tax Breaks for Outsourcing Act. This bill aims to eliminate benefits provided to MNCs provided under the Tax Cuts and Jobs Act of 2017.

9. Made in America tax credits: See #5.

10. Dividends and capital gains: Biden's plan called for raising the capital gains tax from 20 to 24 percent.

11. Social security loophole: Social security benefits are paid by the FICA tax, which is 12.4 percent of pay (split evenly between the employer and the employee). But earnings are taxed only up to a capital rate. In 2021, the *capital* rate was *$142,800*. Eliminating the top capital rate for wealthy people could increase federal revenue by $425.2 billion in nominal dollars over five years and keep the social security solvent for decades.

Speculative Trading on Wall Street

In light of the problems and threats from Wall Street, I think the only thing that might change their speculation and financial engineering is a threat to their profits in the form of taxes on financial transactions. Here are some suggestions:

- A small financial transaction tax (FTT) of 30 cents on $1,000 would generate $350 billion over nine years.
- Derivatives are bets. They create liabilities where none existed before. They are at the heart of the speculative trading system and should be taxed heavily enough under a FTT to discourage their creation when there is no compelling need to hedge

exposure. Derivatives were at the heart of the financial melt-
down in 2008. Other countries are now taxing them. Some
financial analysts suggest a small fee (say, 0.10 percent) on
the sale or purchase of derivatives would be acceptable. The
original Dodd/Frank bill made them illegal, but Wall Street
was able to get them back into their arsenal. Perhaps, the best
solution for both derivatives and credit default swaps would
be for investors to know that the government and taxpayer
wouldn't bail the bank out if they got into trouble.

- Hedge funds: The primary way that the general partners of
  a hedge fund are compensated is through carried interest,
  which is usually around 20 percent of profits accrued above a
  specified *hurdle rate*. Often, the hurdle rate is about 8 percent,
  and thus any returns the fund achieves above that rate means
  the fund's general partners receive a 20 percent commission in
  addition to any profit on assets the partners have personally
  invested in the fund. Both the profits on personal assets and
  carried interest are taxed at a *capital gains* rate, which for
  high-income earners is 20 percent. According to the Institutional Investor's Rich List, the top 25 hedge funds made $32
  billion in 2020 which averages to $1.3 billion per firm.[8] So,
  the tax of 20 percent just doesn't seem appropriate since the
  government needs more revenue and they could certainly
  afford Biden's capital gains tax of 24 percent, but the new tax
  on hedge funds failed in the Senate by one vote.

Training and Skilled Workers

A 2018 study by Deloitte and the Manufacturing Institute predicted
that U.S. manufacturing would have 2.1 million unfilled manufacturing
jobs by 2030. The Deloitte report also says 2.69 million manufacturing workers will be retiring, so the skilled worker shortage is now a fact.
There are not enough skilled workers to offset the retirees, reshore foreign

---

[8] R. Frank. February 22, 2021. "25 Highest-Paid Hedge Fund Managers Made
$32 Billion in 2020," *Institutional Investor's Rich List*, CNBC.

production, much less supply the 556,000 new manufacturing jobs projected by the government for infrastructure.

A January 2020 training survey by the Manufacturing Institute shows that most MNCs have not invested in long-term skilled training like apprentice training programs. The study says that most companies think training is important or very important for their success over the next year, but only 10 percent said they were very ready to address this trend.

Instead of investing in long-term training, MNCs have used stop gap measures such as outsourcing, automation, buying services from foreign vendors, and poaching trained workers from their suppliers; but these strategies no longer work and the shortage of workers has caught up to American companies. If the United States is successful at reshoring manufacturing and jobs, we simply do not have the skilled manufacturing employees to handle reshored work or the new jobs that will be created by the infrastructure bill.

It appears the only answer is going to be a government-funded program to create these new workers as happened during World War II. The request for government funding is already happening in the semiconductor industry where the industry is asking the National Science Foundation for $50 million in matching funds to improve STEM education. But the billions of dollars of funds going to workforce development, training, and education for Biden's American Jobs Plan was to come from new taxes, which have not been approved by Congress.

MNCs are vulnerable: The adoption of the shareholder value, stock prices, and short-term profit strategies by the multinationals, the decline of federal basic research, and the loss of technologies through outsourcing have made the MNCs and the country vulnerable. There is plenty of evidence confirming that outsourcing their products and technologies will eventually cost them both the technologies and the market. I think it is in the interest of America's multinationals to find ways to protect their technologies, reduce outsourcing, and shift their focus to playing in a long-term economic game, if they want to be competitive in the future.

The last 40 years of economic policies have favored wealth over work and corporations over families. President Biden is trying to build a stronger domestic industrial base and to ensure that the future is made in America for American workers and families. He has also tried to ensure that America's

MNCs pay their fair share in taxes and put their workers and communities first rather than their shareholders. But this is a tall order and can only happen if the CEOs follow through with their pledge to help all stakeholders.

Alex Gorsky, the CEO of Johnson & Johnson, stated that their 2019 pledge "better reflects the way corporations can and should operate today. It affirms the essential role corporations can play in improving our society when CEOs are truly committed to all stakeholders." Since 181 CEOs signed the pledge to all stakeholders, then it is up to the managers and supervisors who work for them to make it happen. Upton Sinclair once remarked that "It is difficult to get a man to understand something when his salary depends on not understanding it." So, to achieve the pledge to all stakeholders will require the leaders of these corporations to change the rules so that their subordinate's salary doesn't depend on it.

This book provides a pragmatic analysis of the problems these managers must solve to meet the needs of all stakeholders, including employees, suppliers, communities, and an economy that serves all Americans. It also offers many solutions that will help them improve their job performance.

The future is now.

About the Author

Michael Collins, MBA, has 35 years of experience in manufacturing. Before retiring in 2004, he was vice president and general manager of two divisions of Columbia Machine in Vancouver, WA. His major customers were the S&P 500 multinational corporations, and he worked with them from 1974 to 2004. This experience gave him a firsthand look at America's multinational corporations and their strategies. He was able to watch firsthand the beginning of outsourcing and the focus on short-term profits and shareholder value.

He has written for many industrial trade journals, including *Industry Week* and *Forbes Magazine*. Since September 2007, he has written and published more than 460 articles and columns on a wide variety of topics.

He is also the author of four books:

1. The Manufacturer's Guide to Business Marketing (1994)
2. Saving American Manufacturing (2006)
3. Growth Planning Handbook for Small and Midsize Manufacturers (2006)
4. The Rise of Inequality and the Decline of the Middle Class (2016)

Michael Collins holds an MBA degree from City University and a BS degree from Portland State University in Portland Oregon. He can be reached at mpcmgt.net.

Index

OTHER TITLES IN THE ECONOMICS AND PUBLIC POLICY COLLECTION

Jeffrey Edwards, North Carolina A&T State University, Editor

- *The Future Path of SMEs* by Amr Sukkar
- *Rebooting Local Economies* by Robert Pittman, Rhonda Phillips, and Amanda Sutt
- *The Language of Value* by Virginia B. Robertson
- *Transparency in ESG and the Circular Economy* by Dolan Cristina and Barrero Zalles Diana
- *Developing Sustainable Energy Projects in Emerging Markets* by Francis Ugboma
- *Understanding the Indian Economy from the Post-Reforms of 1991, Volume III* by Shrawan Kumar Singh
- *Understanding Economic Equilibrium* by Mike Shaw, Thomas J. Cunningham, and Rosemary Cunningham
- *Business Liability and Economic Damages, Second Edition* by Scott D. Gilbert
- *Macroeconomics, Third Edition* by David G. Tuerck
- *Negotiation Booster* by Kasia Jagodzinska
- *Mastering the Moneyed Mind, Volume IV* by Christopher Bayer
- *Mastering the Moneyed Mind, Volume III* by Christopher Bayer
- *Mastering the Moneyed Mind, Volume II* by Christopher Bayer
- *Mastering the Moneyed Mind, Volume I* by Christopher Bayer

Concise and Applied Business Books

The Collection listed above is one of 30 business subject collections that Business Expert Press has grown to make BEP a premiere publisher of print and digital books. Our concise and applied books are for...

- Professionals and Practitioners
- Faculty who adopt our books for courses
- Librarians who know that BEP's Digital Libraries are a unique way to offer students ebooks to download, not restricted with any digital rights management
- Executive Training Course Leaders
- Business Seminar Organizers

Business Expert Press books are for anyone who needs to dig deeper on business ideas, goals, and solutions to everyday problems. Whether one print book, one ebook, or buying a digital library of 110 ebooks, we remain the affordable and smart way to be business smart. For more information, please visit www.businessexpertpress.com, or contact sales@businessexpertpress.com.